IN TUNE

BOOK 2

Manuel C. R. dos Santos

Centro Internacional de Línguas
Curitiba, Paraná, Brazil

ScottForesman

A Division of HarperCollinsPublishers

Art by Tom Dunnington.
Cover illustration by Andrea Eberbach.

ISBN: 0-673-19102-8

10-RRC-9796959493

I would like to acknowledge my good fortune in having had such a wonderful team of editors working with me on this project, and a wife like

HELOISA

whose constant encouragement, criticism, and dedication to the program have been a very special kind of "coauthorship."

Thank you, too, my sons, for putting up with me during the three years of writing and composing, and for giving up time which normally would have been yours.

The Author

Contents

v

Using the Cue Book

Student
Book

You will use the Cue Books for
many exercises. Here's how:

Cue Book

---

1. Put the Cue Book
next to your
Student Book.

---

2. Look at the exercise
in the Student Book.

---

3. Open the Cue Book
to the Chart
mentioned in the
exercise directions.

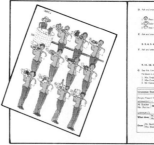 

---

4. Read the directions in the Student Book. Look in the Cue Book to find the picture that has the number mentioned in the directions. (NOTE: We don't always begin with Picture 1.).

Ask and Answer. Use Cue Book Chart 2. Start with **1.** Answer *ad lib*.
    STUDENT A: I don't like tea. Do you?
    STUDENT B: Yes, I do. *or:* No, I don't.

5. Continue, matching the Cue Book pictures with the boldface numbers in the exercise.

Ask and answer. Use Cue Book Chart 2. Start with **1.** Answer *ad lib*.
    STUDENT A: I don't like tea. Do you?
    STUDENT B: Yes, I do. *or:* No, I don't.
    STUDENT C: I don't like coffee. Do you?
    STUDENT D: Yes, I do. *or:* No, I don't.
    STUDENT E: I don't like hamburgers. Do you?
    STUDENT F: . . . etc.

LESSON 1

CONVERSATION

	BOB:	Hi, Joe. Hi, Lily. How are you this evening?
	JOE:	Fine, thanks. Bob, we'd like you to meet a friend of ours from Spain.
	LILY:	Luz! Come here, please.
5	LUZ:	Yes?
	LILY:	Luz, this is Bob Cooper. He's a good friend of ours. Bob, this is Luz Hernandez.
	LUZ:	How do you do?
	BOB:	I'm pleased to meet you. I love Spain. I was
10		there last spring. Where are you from?
	LUZ:	Barcelona. Do you know it?*
	BOB:	No, I'm afraid I don't. I only know Madrid and Toledo. Cigarette?
	LUZ:	No, thank you. I don't smoke.
15	LILY:	It's a lovely party, isn't it?
	LUZ:	Yes, it is, but it's very warm in here.
	JOE:	Would you like something to drink?
	LUZ:	Oh, yes, please. I'd love some orange juice. *(Joe leaves.)* What do you do, Bob?
20	BOB:	I'm a salesman. I sell children's clothes. I live here in New York, but I travel a lot. How about you?
	LUZ:	I'm a teacher.
	LILY:	Luz comes to New York every summer.
	LUZ:	Yes, I like New York very much.
25	BOB:	Well, here's my address and phone number.
	JOE:	And here's your orange juice. Cheers!
	LUZ:	Cheers!
	BOB:	Are you traveling alone?
	LUZ:	No, I'm with my husband. He's over there.
30		Raul! I'd like you to meet Bob . . .
		I'm sorry. What was your last name?
	BOB:	Cooper.
	RAUL:	Nice to meet you, Bob.
	BOB:	Nice to meet you too.

---

*We *meet* people, but not places or things. We *know* people, places, and sometimes things.

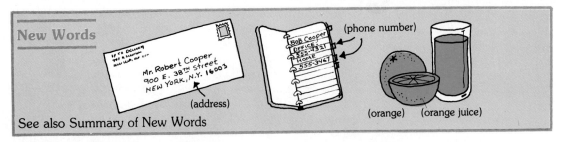

New Words

(phone number)

(address)

(orange)   (orange juice)

See also Summary of New Words

MINI-CONVERSATION 1

A: Hi. How are you?
B: Fine, thanks. And you?
A: Great! Are you alone this evening?
B: No, my wife's with me. I'd like you to meet her.

MINI-CONVERSATION 2

A: I'd like you to meet a friend of mine—Bill Jenkins. Bill, this is John Langly.
B: How do you do, Bill?
C: Pleased to meet you.

CONVERSATION PRACTICE

About the Conversation

1. Is Bob a good friend of Joe and Lily's?   2. Does Bob know Barcelona?   3. Which cities does he know in Spain?   4. Does Luz smoke?   5. What's the party like?   6. What does Luz want to drink?   7. What does she do?   8. Does she come to New York often?   9. Does she like it?   10. Is she traveling alone?   11. What's Bob's last name?

Situation

There is a party at your house. A friend arrives from the U.S. and wants to meet some people. He / She does and you, he / she, and your friends talk. Your friends want to know:

where he / she lives	where he / she is staying
what he / she does	how long he / she is staying
why he / she is in their country	what he / she likes to do
how often he / she comes there	what he'd / she'd like to drink

SUMMARY OF NEW WORDS

AUXILIARY VERBS	NOUNS			
would	address(es)	orange(s)	orange juice	phone number(s)

ADJECTIVES	PRONOUNS + *would*						
alone	I'd	you'd	he'd	she'd	we'd	you'd	they'd

PHRASES AND EXPRESSIONS			
a friend of (mine, yours, his, etc.)	Cheers!	How do you do?	Nice / Pleased to
	How are you?	I'd / We'd like you	meet you.

EXERCISES

A. Ask and answer. Start with *old phone number.*

> STUDENT A: It's an old phone number, isn't it?
> STUDENT B: No, it isn't. It's new.

1. new address
2. heavy suitcase
3. light jacket
4. beautiful watch
5. unattractive dress
6. long time
7. short book
8. thick newspaper
9. thin glass
10. empty box
11. full bottle
12. clean room

B. Use the right word or expression to answer.

1. A: Hi! How are you?
   B: *(I'm fine, thanks. / I'm sorry.)*
2. A: Joe, I'd like you to meet Mr. Smooth.
   B: *(Cheers! / How do you do?)*
3. A: We're waiting for you. Where were you?
   B: *(I'm alone. / I'm sorry I'm late.)*
4. A: We'd like you to meet a friend of ours: Miss Garcia.
   B: *(Pleased to meet you. / Hi!)*
5. A: Here's your glass of wine.
   B: *(Fine, thanks. / Thank you. Cheers!)*
6. A: How are you?
   B: *(Fine, thanks. How are you? / Ah! I'm sorry.)*
7. A: Do you know Yoko?
   B: *(Yes, she's a friend of ours. / Yes, here's my address.)*
8. A: Who's the young woman with you?
   B: *(Nice to meet you. / Her name is Maria. I'd like you to meet her.)*
9. A: I'd like to go to Bob's house.
   B: *(I'm afraid I don't know his address. / I'm afraid I don't know his last name.)*
10. A: How do you do?
    B: *(I'm a doctor. / Pleased to meet you.)*

Grammar Summary

1. Tag Questions

I'm				I?*
You're		aren't	{	you?
He's			{	he?
She's	late,	isn't	{	she?
It's			{	it?
We're			{	we?
You're		aren't	{	you?
They're			{	they?

*NOTE: **I am (I'm)** → **aren't I?***

2. Polite Forms

I'd			I	
You'd			You	
He'd			He	
She'd	**like** . . . =		She	want(s) . . .
We'd			We	
You'd			You	
They'd			They	

DEVELOPING YOUR SKILLS

Complete the conversations.

1. A: ___ you ___ some orange juice?
   B: No, ___. I'm not ___ .
2. A: He needs some money.
   B: How ___ ?
3. A: Do you know her address?
   B: No, but I know her ___ ___ . It's 555-0425.
   A: Is she ___ home tonight?
   B: I ___ she is.
4. A: The children's bedroom is upstairs, ___ ___?
   B: No, it ___ . It's ___ .
5. A: Jerry, ___ like you to ___ Alexandra. She's a good friend of ___ .
   B: Nice ___ ___ ___ . Where ___ ___ from?
   C: From Athens. ___ ___ know ___?
   B: I'm afraid I don't, but ___ love to go there.
6. A: You're going to the bank, ___ ___?
   B: No, ___ ___. Why?
   A: ___ ___ you to ___ this check.
7. A: ___ are you waiting for?
   B: For my son. He's arriving now. ___ ___ like to meet him?
8. A: Are those ___ ?
   B: No, they aren't ours. I think they're Fernando's.
9. A: I'm sick, ___ ___?
   B: I don't ___. ___ don't you ___ a doctor?
10. A: ___ ___ are you staying in our town?
    B: For three days.
11. A: ___ ___ the weather like?
    B: It was very cold.
12. A: Where did Mr. and Mrs. Garcia go ___ night?
    B: They ___ to the theater.

Talk About Yourself

Talk about the last party you went to.

1. Where was it?   2. What did you eat?   3. What did you drink?   4. Was there music? Did you dance?   5. What time did the party start?   6. What time did it finish?   7. Did you meet any interesting people? Who?   8. Did you have a good time?

Complete the conversations. (1 point for each conversation)

1. A: ___ ___ ___ something to eat?
   B: Yes, ___ ___ a turkey sandwich, please.
2. A: Are you ___?
   B: No, I'm with my family.
3. A: What's your ___ ___?
   B: 555-9863.
4. A: Thank you very much for the chocolates.
   B: You're ___.
5. A: Hello. ___ ___ ___ ?
   B: I'm fine, thanks. ___ ___ you?
   A: Fine.
6. A: ___ else?
   B: Yes, please. I'd like some butter.
7. A: I'd like you to meet a friend of mine. Yoko, ___ ___ Bob.
   B: ___ ___ ___ ___ .
8. A: I'm studying a lot, ___ ___ ?
   B: Yes, you are. ___ don't you go to bed?
   A: ___ I have a test tomorrow.
9. A: ___ ___ ___ ___ ?
   B: I'm very pleased to meet you.
10. A: ___ ___ ___ ___ ?
    B: About 7:30.

Total Score _____

LESSON 2

CONVERSATION

STEVE: Hello, darling.

PEGGY: I want to talk to you.

STEVE: Huh? What's the matter?

PEGGY: I'm leaving you.

5   STEVE: You're what!?

PEGGY: I'm afraid it's no good. It's the same thing
every day. You get up, take your shower, have
breakfast, and read your newspaper . . . You
never talk to me.

10   STEVE: I always talk to you, darling.

PEGGY: Oh, no, you don't. You didn't talk to me this
morning or yesterday or the day before yesterday. And we never go out either.

STEVE: But we went out . . .

15   PEGGY: Two months ago!

STEVE: Well, I work very hard. I start early and finish
late. This morning I started at seven-thirty.

PEGGY: I work hard too, you know. I start early and
never finish. And you never help me. This

20   morning I got up before you, made breakfast,
took the children to school, and went to work.
After work I picked up the children, came home,
cooked your dinner, and then waited for you.
Where were you?

25   STEVE: I was at the office. I had an important
meeting today. I thought you knew.

PEGGY: No, I didn't.

STEVE: I'm sorry, darling. Really I am. Look!
Why don't we go to Giovanni's tomorrow

30   night and have a nice Italian dinner,
and then go dancing at the Rendezvous?

PEGGY: Oh, Steve, sometimes I just hate you . . .

New Words

(to help / helped)

(to call / called)

(to look after / looked after)

(to pick up / picked up)

(to get / got)

MINI-CONVERSATION 1

A: Are things still the same between you and Peggy?
B: No, I'm afraid it's just no good. Peggy left me.
A: She what!?
B: She left me the day before yesterday.

MINI-CONVERSATION 2

A: Does Abdul write often?
B: Rarely. I think the last letter I got was about a year ago. He always forgets to write. But I spoke to him on the phone last week. He called from Beirut.
A: Really? How is he?
B: He's very well, but working hard. He sends his regards.

MINI-CONVERSATION 3

A: Now, when did you last see this man?
B: Last month, officer. He came to the bank and cashed a check. Then he wanted to sell some watches.
A: Do people normally come to the bank to sell watches?
B: No, never.
A: Then why didn't you report it to the police?
B: I guess I forgot.

MINI-CONVERSATION 4

A: Did you pick up your clothes?
B: Oh, no! I'm afraid I forgot.
A: I need help around the house. I cook, clean, look after the children . . .
B: I'm sorry, darling. Really I am.

CONVERSATION PRACTICE

About the Conversation

1. Is Peggy happy?   2. What does she want to do?   3. Does Steve talk to Peggy in the morning?   4. What did he do yesterday morning?   5. Do they go out often?   6. When did they last go out?   7. Who got up first this morning?   8. What did Peggy do when she came home?   9. Where was Steve?   10. What didn't Peggy know about?   11. Is Steve sorry?   12. What's his idea for tomorrow night?   13. Do you think Peggy is going out with Steve tomorrow or is she really leaving him?

Situation 1

You arrive home tired. Your husband / wife / friend wants to go out.

Say you are tired. You worked very hard.
> Your husband / wife / friend wants to go out.

You want to stay home and go to bed early.
> Your husband / wife / friend works hard too and sometimes likes to go out and have a good time.

You talk about your day.
> Your husband / wife / friend does too and talks about his / her plans for the evening.

You argue with him / her.

Situation 2

You are calling a friend to talk to him / her about a post card you got.

Say who is speaking.
> Your friend asks how you are.

Answer and tell him / her you got a post card from . . . *(name of person)* in . . . *(name of place)*.
> Your friend wants to know how he / she is, what he / she is doing, does he / she like the place, about his / her job and family.

Tell him / her.

SUMMARY OF NEW WORDS

NEW VERBS: REGULAR

to call / called   to help / helped   to pick up / picked up
to go dancing / went dancing   to look (after) / looked (after)

NEW VERBS: IRREGULAR

to forget / forgot[1]   to get / got[2]   to send / sent

NEW PAST TENSES: REGULAR

to cash / cashed   to fish / fished   to smoke / smoked   to want / wanted
to cook / cooked   to listen (to) / listened (to)   to start / started   to work / worked
to dance / danced   to report / reported   to talk / talked

NEW PAST TENSES: IRREGULAR

to get up / got up   to know / knew   to make / made   to put on / put on   to sell / sold

NOUNS			OBJECT PRONOUNS	ADJECTIVES	
darling	the police	regards	you *(sing.)*	same	well

ADVERBS

ago   hard   never   rarely
(the) day before yesterday   last   normally   really

PHRASES AND EXPRESSIONS

I('m), You('re), etc., what!?   It's no good.   Look!   to send your regards   you know

---

[1]To forge**t** → forgetting.
[2]To ge**t** → getting.

EXERCISES

A. Ask and answer. Use Cue Book Chart 1. Start with *first / 9 / chess / about a year ago.*

> STUDENT A: When did you first play chess?
> STUDENT B: I first played chess about a year ago.

1. last / **10** / in the shower / about a week ago
2. last / **11** / in this armchair / about two months ago
3. last / **12** / in a hotel / on my vacation
4. first / **13** / a cigarette / when I was a boy (girl)
5. last / **14** / to your daughter / about two hours ago
6. last / **15** / in the rain / when I went to work this morning
7. first / **16** / to the president / when he was at our factory
8. last / **17** / for a friend at the airport / about a year ago
9. last / **18** / to work / the day before yesterday
10. first / **19** / in a department store / when I lived in England

B. Ask and answer. Use Cue Book Chart 1. Start with *what / 20 / I / about / the Italian market.*

> STUDENT A: What did you write about?
> STUDENT B: I wrote about the Italian market.

1. What / **1** / about / we / about the style of the building
2. Where / **2** / we / at the Rendezvous
3. What / **3** / I / beer
4. Where / **4** / to / I / to the city
5. When / **5** / we / at noon
6. Where / **6** / I / in the river nearby
7. What / **7** / we / Greek music
8. What / **8** / we / some new shirts
9. What / **9** / I / golf
10. Where / **10** / we / in the theater

C. Put the verbs in the past tense.

1. The Reeds *(to sell)* their house because they *(to need)* the money.
2. I *(to look after)* the children because their parents *(to want)* to go out.
3. The poor people *(to get)* food and clothes when they *(to leave)*.
4. I *(to send)* post cards to all my friends when I *(to be)* in China last year.
5. He *(to put on)* his new suit because he *(to have)* an important meeting.
6. Mary *(to help)* her father in the office yesterday.
7. The woman *(to pick up)* the old newspapers, but she *(to forget)* to put them in the box.
8. She *(to make)* a new dress, *(to buy)* a new hat, and *(to get)* some new shoes.
9. When Mr. Panos *(to see)* the thief he *(to pick up)* the phone and *(to call)* the police.
10. But, darling, I *(to think)* you *(to know)* about the party.

Grammar Summary

1. Adverbs of Frequency   *2. Adverb of Time: Ago*

I You He She It We You They	**always** **usually** **often** **normally** **sometimes** **rarely** **never**	eat(s) / ate fish.

I You He She It We You They	**ate** fish two days **ago**.

NOTE: We use **ago** only with the past tense.

DEVELOPING YOUR SKILLS

Write the correct form of the verb: simple present or simple past.

1. Alice rarely *(to write)* to her mother, but today she *(to speak)* to her on the phone.
2. Fred never *(to get up)* early when he was a student, but now he always *(to leave)* the house before eight o'clock.
3. I usually *(to prefer)* to stay home when the weather was cold.
4. We rarely work late, but last night we *(to finish)* at eleven o'clock.
5. Maria normally helps her mother in the house and then she *(to go)* to school.
6. When we were children we sometimes *(to make)* and *(to sell)* cakes to our friends.

Reading

Peggy normally looks after the house and the children. But the day before yesterday she took a trip with her sister and Steve stayed at home with the children. Yesterday he got up early, drank a cup of coffee and some orange juice, and cooked breakfast. The children loved it and they ate a lot. Steve likes to cook, but he rarely does it. After breakfast they left the house to go
5   to work and school. They put on heavy sweaters and coats because it was very cold. The car didn't start and Steve was really angry. He called a taxi, but they still arrived late.

The children usually eat lunch at school and they did that yesterday too. Steve normally has lunch in his office, but yesterday he didn't have anything to eat. He just didn't have time. He had a really busy day and worked very hard.
10   At about 6:30 Peggy called him at the office:

PEGGY: Hello, darling. This is Peggy. What's the matter? I called home, but you weren't there. Where are the children?

STEVE: Oh, no! I forgot! They're still at school.

1. Who usually looks after the children and the house?   2. Why didn't she look after the house and children the day before yesterday?   3. When did Steve get up yesterday?   4. Does Steve like to cook?   5. Does he cook often?   6. Why did they put on thick sweaters and coats? 7. Why did they call a taxi?   8. When did they arrive at work and school?   9. Did Steve eat lunch yesterday? Why not?   10. Did he work hard?   11. Did you work hard yesterday? 12. When did Peggy call Steve?   13. What did Steve forget to do?

Talk About Yourself

1. Do you like to look after children? Why?   2. Do you often call your friends? What do you usually talk about?   3. When did you last call a friend? What did you talk about?   4. Do you get many letters? When did you last get one? Who was the letter from?   5. Do you often write letters? Who do you write to? When did you last write a letter?

Test Yourself

Make sentences. (2 points each)

know / cars / they / I / didn't / there / made   *I didn't know they made cars there.*

1. got up / normally / yesterday / but / late / we / get up / we / early
2. good / last / did / book / you / read / when / a
3. phone / have / a / her / called / rarely / parents / they / because / didn't / Peggy's
4. I / some / forgot / potatoes / afraid / to buy / I'm
5. newspapers / sold / Kiku / interesting / to / the / story / very / a   Total Score _____

What to say . . .

...and give my regards to your mother.

LESSON 3

CONVERSATION 1

MRS. DUKE: Hello.
TV ANNOUNCER: Is this Mrs. Duke at 613 Bramley Street?
MRS. DUKE: Yes, that's right.
TV ANNOUNCER: Are you watching television, Mrs. Duke?
MRS. DUKE: Yes, I am.
TV ANNOUNCER: May I ask what channel?
MRS. DUKE: Thirteen.
TV ANNOUNCER: Good! This is Bob Taylor at Channel 13. Do you often watch my show?
MRS. DUKE: Oh, yes. We always watch your show. My husband and I enjoy it very much.
TV ANNOUNCER: Is he watching with you?
MRS. DUKE: No, I'm afraid he's taking a bath now.
TV ANNOUNCER: May I ask what soap he normally uses?
MRS. DUKE: I only buy Brand X. We use it all the time.
TV ANNOUNCER: Great! Now, Mrs. Duke, may I ask where you and your husband are going on vacation this year?
MRS. DUKE: Oh, it's too expensive to travel nowadays.
TV ANNOUNCER: Well, not this year, Mrs. Duke. Brand X soap is giving you and Mr. Duke a trip to the Greek islands and 4,000 Q. Congratulations!
MRS. DUKE: They're giving us a trip? Terrific!

CONVERSATION 2

TRAVEL AGENT: Here are your tickets and passports. Now don't forget them. And please check in early and go through passport control immediately.
MRS. DUKE: Are there many people on this flight?
TRAVEL AGENT: Yes, it's full, because it lands in Paris first and then goes to Athens.
MR. DUKE: What time does the plane take off?
TRAVEL AGENT: It takes off at 11:30, but it usually boards forty-five minutes before.
MRS. DUKE: And what time do we get to Athens?
TRAVEL AGENT: Seven o'clock in the morning. Have a pleasant trip.
MR. DUKE: Oh, yes! We're *very* excited.

New Words

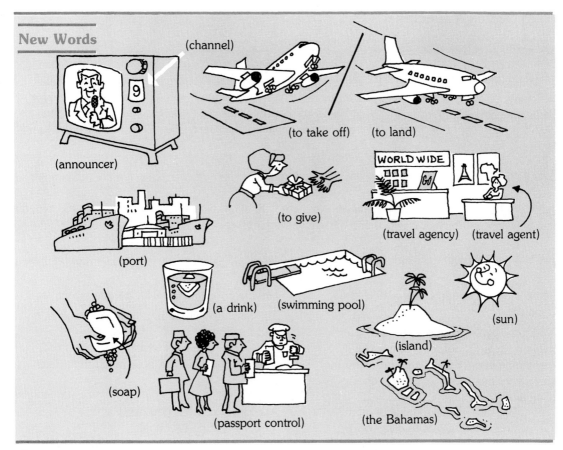

(channel)

(to take off) (to land)

(announcer)

(to give)

(travel agency) (travel agent)

(port)

(a drink) (swimming pool)

(sun)

(island)

(soap)

(passport control) (the Bahamas)

MINI-CONVERSATION 1

A: May I ask what you did before you boarded?

B: Oh, I just mailed some post cards and bought a package of duty-free cigarettes. Of course I was very excited about the trip.

MINI-CONVERSATION 2

A: When I looked through the window I saw a man in my bedroom.

B: What did you do?

A: I opened the door and went in immediately.

B: I guess he ran when he saw you.

A: No, he didn't. He hugged and kissed me.

B: He hugged and kissed you?!

A: Yes, it was my father.

MINI-CONVERSATION 3

A: How was your cruise to the Bahamas?

B: I really enjoyed it. First we flew to Miami and then took the boat to Nassau and Freeport. Nassau is the capital of the islands and the main city.

A: What was it like on the boat?

B: It was very pleasant. We swam, rested, they gave us good food and drinks—and it never rained. I'm afraid the sun was too hot for George. He wore his hat and shirt all the time. But I think he enjoyed the trip too.

CONVERSATION PRACTICE

About Conversation 1

1. Where do the Dukes live?   2. What channel does Mrs. Duke normally watch?   3. Is she watching it now?   4. Do the Dukes enjoy the Bob Taylor Show?   5. Who is Bob?   6. Is Mr. Duke watching TV? Why?   7. What brand of soap does he use?   8. How about you? What brand do you use?   9. Why aren't the Dukes traveling this year?   10. What did they get from Brand X soap?

About Conversation 2

Ask: 1. about the number of people on this flight.   2. what time the plane takes off.   3. where it flies to first.   4. when it gets there.   5. how long it takes.

Situation 1

Have a phone conversation with a radio announcer.

You are listening to the show but your husband / wife is not. He / She is doing something else. *(Say what)* You enjoy the show very much, but you don't always listen. *(Say why)*

    Because you like the show the announcer wants to give you a package of five new records.

Tell him / her what records you'd like to have.

Situation 2

Have a conversation with a travel agent.

Tell him / her where and how you want to go and for how long.
    He / She asks when.
Tell him / her and ask how much the tickets are.
    He / She tells you.
Ask him / her what you need.
    He / She tells you.
Ask when the plane takes off and lands.
    He / She tells you.
Ask what time you need to be at the airport to board the plane.
    He / She tells you.

SUMMARY OF NEW WORDS

<u>NEW VERBS: REGULAR</u>
to enjoy / enjoyed   to land / landed   to use / used*

<u>NEW VERBS: IRREGULAR</u>
to get to / got to   to give / gave*   to go in / went in   to take off / took off*

<u>NEW PAST TENSES: REGULAR</u>

to board / boarded	to hug / hugged	to like / liked	to open / opened	to rent / rented
to check in / checked in	to kiss / kissed	to mail / mailed	to rain / rained	to rest / rested

---

*Don't forget: to us**e** → us**ing**, to giv**e** → giv**ing**, to tak**e** off → tak**ing** off.

EXERCISES

A. Ask and answer. Use Cue Book Chart 1. Start with *who / you* (sing.) / **16** / *to? / announcer.*

> STUDENT A: Who are you talking to?
> STUDENT B: I'm talking to the announcer.

1. Who / Mrs. Tanaka / **17** / for? / travel agent
2. Where / James and Ali / **18**? / on the island
3. Why / you *(sing.)* / **19** / late? / I have a lot of work to do
4. What / Mrs. Duke / **20** / about? / her cruise
5. Who / Mr. Grump / **1** / with? / the passport control officer
6. Where / Mike and Susan / **2**? / at the nightclub
7. What / Abdul / **3**? / milk
8. When / Maria / **4** / to Greece? / next week
9. Why / Fernando and Sophia / **5** / potatoes? / there isn't anything else
10. Where / the children / **6**? / on the boat

B. Ask and answer. Use Cue Book Chart 1. Start with *you* (sing.) / **7** / *the music / it's too quiet for me.*

> STUDENT A: Why aren't you listening to the music?
> STUDENT B: Because it's too quiet for me.

1. Mr. Baker / **8** / a swimsuit / the sun is too hot for him
2. Mr. and Mrs. Rodriguez / **9** / golf / it's too windy for them
3. Alexandra / **10** / with her friends / she's too sleepy
4. Mr. Angelo / **11** / on the chair / it's too small for him
5. Concepcion / **12** / in her bedroom / too cold for her
6. you *(pl.)* / **13** / today / bad for us
7. Pierre and Ingrid / **14** / to you / they're very angry

C. Choose the correct form of the verb.

1. We loved the chocolate Mary *(gave, gives, is giving)* us.
2. I usually *(am enjoying, enjoyed, enjoy)* the shows we see on Channel 5 every day.

3. Toshiro *(flies, is flying, flew)* to Hong Kong tomorrow.
4. My sister always *(uses, is using, used)* my soap when she takes a bath.
5. Yoko *(is, are, were)* very excited because she just *(is going, goes, went)* to the travel agency.
6. The plane didn't *(took off, take off, to take off)* because of the bad weather.
7. Now, gentlemen, the main thing for salesmen *(is, was, were)* to be pleasant with the customers.
8. How much money *(is, do, does)* a bus driver *(get, gets, got)?*
9. The pilot was still on the plane when he *(to see, saw, is seeing)* his wife.
10. Why *(aren't, isn't, wasn't)* you buying any duty-free products?

Grammar Summary

1. Frequency Adverbs vs. Adverbs of Time

<u>FREQUENCY</u>   <u>TIME</u>

I **usually go** to Rome on my vacation every summer, but **this year I'm going** to Athens.
We **normally watch** the Bob Taylor Show in the morning, but **today we're watching**
 Tea for Two.

We usually use frequency adverbs with the simple present and adverbs of time with the present progressive.

2. Subject Pronouns / Object Pronouns   *3. May I ask . . . ?*

I / me	**we / us**
you / you	**you / you**
he / him	**they / them**
she / her	
it / it	

Where are you going on your vacation?
May I ask where you are going on your vacation?

Which soap **does he** normally **use?**
May I ask which soap **he** normally **uses?**

Why did you walk to the port?
May I ask why you walked to the port?

DEVELOPING YOUR SKILLS

A. Use the correct pronouns.

> *Mary and I* saw *the thief* but he didn't see *Mary and me*.
> We saw him, but he didn't see us.

1. I spoke to *Mrs. Graham*, but *Mrs. Graham* didn't speak to me.
2. *Alexandra* called *Pete*, but *Pete* didn't talk to *Alexandra*.
3. *Jack and I* knew *their children*, but *their children* didn't know *Jack and me*.
4. *John* always listened to *Mary*, but *Mary* never listened to *John*.
5. *My friends* never wrote to me, but I always wrote to *my friends*.
6. *Mary* often helps you, but *Mary* never helps *her father*.
7. *Our son* normally uses *our car*, but *our son* rarely takes *the car* to the garage.

8. I usually argue with *my wife*, but today *my wife* argued with me.
9. I wrote a letter to *you and your father*, but I guess *you and your father* didn't get *the letter*.

B. Ask these questions using *May I ask*.

1. What time are you leaving?
2. Why are you giving us these tickets?
3. When are they going on the cruise?
4. Where's the soap?
5. Why was he next to the swimming pool?
6. When does the plane land?
7. What time do we get to Freeport?
8. Which channel are they watching?
9. Why did you fly?
10. What did she wear on the boat?

C. Complete the letter using these words. Put verbs in the past tense.

| to be | to fly | to have | pleasant | to speak | to talk |
| to check in | to get | to land | to sit | to take off | through |

Dear Martha and Bill,

We . . . a wonderful flight. When we arrived at the airport we . . . , went . . . passport control and then . . . in the departure lounge for about an hour. The plane boarded at 10:45 and . . . at 11:30. Dad and I . . . very excited. We . . . next to a very . . . young man from Crete. He . . . English very well and we . . . for hours. First we . . . to Paris and then to Athens. We . . . early and . . . to the hotel at nine o'clock this morning, tired but happy.

Love,
Mom

Reading

The Dukes got to Athens three days ago and are staying in a beautiful modern hotel. They are having a wonderful time. Yesterday they rented a car and drove to Olympia, the home of the Olympic Games. They didn't go out this morning because they were too tired. They sat in the sun and swam in the hotel swimming pool. This afternoon they went to the Acropolis and saw
5 the Parthenon.
At home the Dukes don't usually go out very much, but here they go out every night. Tonight they are having drinks with some people they met in the hotel. Mrs. Duke is wearing a beautiful new dress and Bliss perfume. Mr. Duke is wearing a new suit and a brand new watch.* He bought the perfume and the watch duty-free at the airport in Paris. Mr. and Mrs. Duke are
10 very excited because tomorrow they are going on a cruise to the islands. They are leaving from Piraeus, the main port, early in the morning.
The Dukes are enjoying their vacation very much. Their travel agent was right. Greece is a great place for a sunny vacation.

---

*NOTE: You *wear* perfume and watches.

About the Reading

Ask the Dukes: 1. when they got to Athens.   2. where they are staying.   3. where they drove to yesterday.   4. what is interesting about Mount Olympus.   5. why they didn't go out this morning.   6. where they are going tonight.   7. who they are going with.   8. what Mr. Duke bought in Paris.   9. where they are going tomorrow.   10. about the weather in Greece.

Talk About Yourself

1. Do you often watch TV?   2. What shows do you prefer? Why? What channel are they on?   3. Are there radio or TV shows in your country where they give things to people? What do they give?   4. Do you live on an island? Do you know any islands? Which ones?   5. Would you like to go to the Greek islands or the Bahamas? Why?

Test Yourself

Choose the correct object pronoun. (1 point each)

1. I don't like oranges very much, but I eat *(it, them)*.
2. Pete and I saw the Joneses in the Bahamas, but they didn't see *(them, us)*.
3. My teacher always helps Jane, but she rarely helps *(me, I)*.
4. Mrs. Brown doesn't usually watch Bob Taylor's show, but today she's watching *(it, them)*.
5. Mr. Grump doesn't like me, and I don't like *(him, her)* much either.

Now choose the correct adjective. (1 point each)

6. John is *(pleasant, weak, excited)* because he's going on a cruise.
7. My father was very *(fat, thin, tall)* because he ate too much.
8. The vegetables in the market were always *(cool, fresh, duty-free)*.
9. Helen wanted something to drink because she was very *(sick, thirsty, hungry)*.
10. At home we like to drink *(strong, young, new)* coffee.

Total Score _____

What to say . . .

May I ask where you got that?

D
Sometimes I'm happy
Em
And sometimes I'm blue
A7
I always feel sad
D
When I don't hear from you
Bm
5   I think every day
Em
Of a table for two
A7
I'm sitting alone
D
And I'm thinking of you.

D
10   I'm always lonely
Em
When you aren't with me
A7
I sit in my room
D
And turn on the TV
Bm
As I watch the show
Em
There's one thing I know
A7
15   I'm thinking of you
D   D7
Are you thinking of me?

G
You're always on my mind
D
When you're far or near
A7
You know my love is blind
D   D7
20   When I have you here
G
It's cold and dark outside
D
And I am staying home
A7
I'm feeling very sad
D
'Cause I'm on my own.

LESSON 4

CONVERSATION 1

ERIC: Happy birthday, Carol.
CAROL: You didn't forget.
ERIC: Of course not. And I brought something for you.
CAROL: Oh! What a beautiful dress! It's just what I wanted.
5   I want to wear it tonight.
ERIC: Where would you like to go?
CAROL: Anywhere!
ERIC: No, not just anywhere. Let's go somewhere special.
       If you're really hungry, let's go to the Limelight.
10   CAROL: I love to eat out, but that's too expensive.
ERIC: But today is a special day.

CONVERSATION 2

WAITER: Good evening, sir . . . ma'am. Can I take your order?
ERIC: Yes, please. My wife would like a shrimp cocktail
       for a first course and I'd like some melon.
WAITER: And for the main course?
5   CAROL: I'd like the roast duck.
WAITER: And for you, sir?
ERIC: The steak, please.
WAITER: Fried or broiled, sir?
ERIC: Broiled, please.
10   WAITER: How would you like it?
ERIC: Medium. And could you also bring us a tomato salad?
WAITER: Certainly, sir.
CAROL: Excuse me. Instead of duck, I think I'd like the veal.
WAITER: Very good, ma'am. And what would you like to drink?
15   ERIC: We'd like a nice bottle of red wine—Bacchus, if you have it.

● ● ●

ERIC: Waiter! Could you bring me the bill, please?
WAITER: Here you are, sir.
ERIC: Darling, did you bring any money?
CAROL: Any what?
20   ERIC: Money. I'm afraid I don't have enough.

(melon)

(tomato)

(mushroom)

(onion)

(lettuce)

(peas)

(shrimp)

(carrot)

(duck)

(shrimp cocktail)

(steak)

(sauce)

(veal)

(boiled)

(fried)

(broiled)

(hand)

(roast(ed))

(bread)

(French fries / French fried potatoes)

(spoon)   (fork)   (knife)

(rice pudding)

January 1, 1900–December 31, 1999

(century)

(chopsticks)

(the same)

(different)

(snake)

(poison)

(snails)

(bill)

MINI-CONVERSATION 1

A: How old are you?
B: Twenty-five.
A: When is your birthday?
B: Today.
A: This *is* a special day. Happy Birthday!

MINI-CONVERSATION 2

A: Can I take your order, sir?
B: Yes, please. I'd like the lamb.
A: Rare, medium, or well-done?
B: Rare. And I'd also like some French fries.
A: Certainly, sir.

MINI-CONVERSATION 3

A: Let's go somewhere.
B: No, I don't want to go anywhere. I want to finish all of this work.

MINI-CONVERSATION 4

A: Mom, could you bring me some rice pudding?
B: I'm afraid there isn't any. Would you like something else instead?
A: Yes, I'd like an orange. But there's only one.
B: Take it if you want it.

MINI-CONVERSATION 5

A: Why didn't you make a birthday cake for Pete?
B: Because I didn't have enough butter and you weren't here to buy any. I really had my hands full.*

CONVERSATION PRACTICE

About Conversation 1

Ask: 1. Eric where he was. 2. what he brought. 3. Carol where she would like to go tonight. 4. what she thinks of the Limelight. 5. Eric why today is a special day.

About Conversation 2

1. What would Carol like to eat? 2. What would Eric like to eat? 3. What would Carol like for the main course? 4. How would Eric like his steak? 5. What kind of salad do they want? 6. What kind of wine would they like? 7. What doesn't Eric have?

---

*To have your hands full = to be very busy.

The Limelight Menu

First Course

Shrimp cocktail	235 Q	Tomato soup	120 Q
Snails	260 Q	French onion soup	160 Q
	Fresh melon	150 Q	

Main Course

Chicken in red wine sauce with onions	330 Q
Roast duck with orange sauce	370 Q
Veal with cheese sauce	420 Q
Lamb with mushrooms and rice	400 Q
Steak (broiled or fried)	445 Q
Fried shrimp	445 Q
Broiled shrimp with rice	470 Q

Vegetables

peas, carrots, broiled tomatoes, rice, or potatoes (boiled or French fried)

Desserts

Rice pudding	95 Q
Ice cream with chocolate sauce	120 Q
Chocolate cake	180 Q
Cheesecake	195 Q

Drinks

French wine (red or white)	275 Q
German beer	130 Q
Coffee or tea	45 Q

Situation 1

You are at the Limelight. The waiter is taking your order.

He asks what you want for a first course.
    Tell him.
He asks about the main course, salad, vegetables.
    Tell him.
He asks what you would like to drink.
    Tell him.

     . . .

    You ask for dessert and for your bill.
He brings it.
    You don't have enough money.

Situation 2

You and a friend are making plans for a birthday party for a third person. Talk about:

The menu / what the person likes to eat.
What you and your friend want to make / bring / buy for the party.
Do you want a large party or a small one?
Where? When? What time?
Who is coming?
Any music?

SUMMARY OF NEW WORDS

<u>VERBS: IRREGULAR</u>

to bring / brought   to eat out / ate out

<u>PRONOUNS</u>

all (of)

<u>CONJUNCTIONS</u>

if

<u>NOUNS</u>

bill(s)	chopstick(s)	knife (knives)	peas	snail(s)
birthday(s)	course(s)	lettuce	poison	snake(s)
bread	duck	melon(s)	pudding	spoon(s)
carrot(s)	fork(s)	menu(s)	sauce(s)	steak(s)
century (centuries)	French fries	mushroom(s)	shrimp*	tomato(es)
cheesecake(s)	hand(s)	onion(s)	shrimp cocktail(s)	veal

<u>ADJECTIVES</u>

boiled	different	fried	rare	special
broiled	enough	medium	roast(ed)	well-done

<u>ADVERBS</u>   <u>PREPOSITIONS</u>

also   anywhere   certainly   instead   somewhere   instead of

<u>PHRASES AND EXPRESSIONS</u>

Can I take your order?	Happy birthday	Let's (not)
Could you . . . ?	How old . . . ?	to have your hands full

---

*NOTE: Shrimp is singular and plural.

EXERCISES

A. Ask and answer. Use Cue Book Chart 2. Start with **11 / 12**.

> STUDENT A: Could you bring me some duck, please?
> STUDENT B: I'm afraid there isn't any. Would you like some
> steak instead?
> STUDENT A: Yes, I would, please. *or:* No, thank you.

1. **13 / 14** 2. **15 / 16** 3. **17 / 18** 4. **1 / 2** 5. **3 / 4** 6. **5 / 6** 7. **7 / 8** 8. **9 / 10**

B. Say with a friend. Use Cue Book Chart 2. Start with **3 / 4**.

> STUDENT A: Let's have some peas.
> STUDENT B: No, instead of peas, I'd like carrots.

1. **5 / 6** 2. **7 / 8** 3. **9 / 10** 4. **11 / 12** 5. **13 / 14** 6. **15 / 16** 7. **17 / 18** 8. **1 / 2**

C. Use the right word or expression to answer.

1. A: How do you like your steak?
   B: *(Rare. / Special, please.)*
2. A: Are there any snakes in your yard?
   B: *(No, but there are shrimp. / No, but there are snails.)*
3. A: How are you?
   B: *(Twenty-three. / Fine, thanks.)*
4. A: Did you enjoy your lunch, ma'am?
   B: *(Yes, thank you. Now I'd like to see a menu, please. / Yes, thank you. Now I'd like my bill, please.)*
5. A: Waiter! Could you please bring some butter for the bread?
   B: *(Yes, I'm here. / Yes, here you are.)*
6. A: Why are you eating with your hands?
   B: *(Because I don't have a knife and fork. / Because I don't have any peas and carrots.)*
7. A: Would you like a first course?
   B: *(Yes, melon for me and poison for my wife. / Yes, potato soup for me and a shrimp cocktail for my wife.)*
8. A: Would you like some dessert?
   B: *(Yes, I'd like cheesecake. / Yes, I'd like chopsticks.)*
9. A: I'd also like some mushrooms.
   B: *(Anywhere else? / Anything else?)*
10. A: That little girl didn't eat all of her dinner.
    B: *(I guess there wasn't enough for her. / I guess there was too much for her.)*
11. A: Let's watch a different show tonight.
    B: *(No, I want to watch the same one we always watch. / Yes, I just love that show.)*
12. A: I'd like to look at that sweater, please, Miss.
    B: *(Certainly. / You what!?)*

Grammar Summary

1. *Would / Wouldn't*

QUESTION (?)						AFFIRMATIVE (+)		
Who						**I'd**	*(I + would)*	
What		I				**You'd**	*(you + would)*	
Why		you				**He'd**	*(he + would)*	
Where		he				**She'd**	*(she + would)*	like . . .
When	**would**	she	like . . . ?			**It'd**	*(it + would)*	
Which		it				**We'd**	*(we + would)*	
How		we				**You'd**	*(you + would)*	
How long		you				**They'd**	*(they + would)*	
How much		they						
How many								

QUESTION (?)				SHORT ANSWER (+)				SHORT ANSWER (−)		
	I				I				I	
	you				you				you	
	he				he				he	
Would	she	like . . . ?	Yes,		she	**would.**	No,		she	**wouldn't.**
	it				it				it	*(would + not)*
	we				we				we	
	you				you				you	
	they				they				they	

NOTE: You answer *I wouldn't* for things you don't want to do. But when a person wants to give you something, you usually say *No, thank you:*

> A: **Would** you like to work today?
> B: **No, I wouldn't.**
but: A: **Would** you like some candy?
> B: **No, thank you.** (*or:* No, I wouldn't, thanks. I'd prefer . . .)

2. *Plural Commands:* Let's

You (don't) want to do something with someone. You say:

> A: **Let's** (not) go downtown.
> B: (+) Yes, **let's.** *or:* (−) No, **let's not.**

DEVELOPING YOUR SKILLS

Ask and answer.

> A: What would you *(sing.)* like to listen to? (guitar music)
> B: I'd like to listen to guitar music.

1. What would Noriko like to bring? (some cheesecake)
2. What would Jack and Abdul like to have? (peas and carrots)
3. What would Ms. Melody like to cook for the party? (veal)
4. When would you *(pl.)* like to get up? (at 7 A.M.)
5. Which dress would Ann like to wear? (the blue one)
6. What would you *(sing.)* like to do on your birthday? (something special)
7. What would you *(sing.)* like to know? (the time, please)
8. What would Mr. Barnes like to know about the sixteenth century? (the clothes they wore)
9. When would you *(sing.)* like to eat out? (tomorrow night)
10. When would the pilot like to leave? (immediately)

Reading

   We all love food. Meat, vegetables, fruit—we enjoy all of them. We like big dinners and light snacks. Nowadays we often just have a sandwich because we don't always have a lot of time. In the eighteenth century, the Earl of Sandwich (1718–1792) didn't have much time either. He loved to play cards and didn't like to leave the card table to go to the dinner table and eat.
5 He had some meat between two pieces[1] of bread and played cards at the same time. He was the father of our modern sandwich.
   We normally eat sandwiches with our hands. Some people always eat with their hands. The Japanese and Chinese use chopsticks. People started to eat with forks in Italy in the sixteenth century. Before that they ate with two knives.
10 We sometimes like to eat out with friends. It is pleasant and we enjoy it. But nowadays it is also very important for business people. They often prefer to do their work in a quiet restaurant instead of in their offices.
   The different kinds of food people eat are also very interesting. In Hong Kong they eat snake; in Japan they eat raw[2] fish; in France they eat snails. In some countries, people eat
15 people!
   Do you like raw fish, snake, or snails? Well, there's an English expression: "One man's meat is another[3] man's poison."

---

[1] a piece of bread;  two pieces of bread.

[2] Raw = not boiled, broiled, fried, or roasted.

[3] This is one man: ; this is another man:

1. Why didn't the Earl of Sandwich want to eat dinner?   2. What did he have instead?
3. When did he live?   4. Do you prefer big lunches and dinners or light snacks? Why?
5. What kinds of sandwiches do you like?   6. When did people start to eat with forks? Where? What did they use before that?   7. What do they use in Japan and China?   8. What do you use?   9. Why do business people sometimes like to do their work in restaurants?   10. Where do they eat snake, raw fish, and snails? Do you eat them? Do you like them or do you think you would like them?   11. Use different words to explain (tell about) "one man's meat is another man's poison."

Talk About Yourself

1. What kind of food do you like?   2. Do you have good restaurants in your city?   3. Do you eat any special foods in your country? Which ones?   4. Do you take business people to restaurants? Why?   5. Do you like to eat out? When did you last eat out? Where? Who was with you?   6. When is your birthday? Did you have a party for your last birthday? Did you have a birthday cake? Did you have a good time? What did you get for your birthday?

Test Yourself

Ask. (2 points each)

1. Ask the waiter to bring a menu.
2. Tell the waiter what you'd like (a first course, a main course, a vegetable, and dessert).
3. Your friend wants steak. How does he want it?
4. You want a bottle of white wine. Ask the waiter what kinds they have.
5. They don't have enough things on the menu. Tell your friend why you prefer a different restaurant.

Total Score _____

What to say . . .

LESSON 5

CONVERSATION 1

MR. BASS: Good morning. I'm looking for Mr. Williams. Could you tell me where his office is?

RECEPTIONIST: Yes. You go down this corridor, turn left at the stairs, and it's the third door on the right.

● ● ●

5   MR. BASS: Are you Mr. Williams?

MR. WILLIAMS: Yes, I'm Paul Williams.

MR. BASS: Oh, I'm afraid I have the wrong person. I'm looking for Mr. Jack Williams.

MR. WILLIAMS: Jack works on the third floor. Many people
10   make the same mistake.

CONVERSATION 2

DRIVER: Excuse me! Could you tell me how to get to the university?

STUDENT: Sure! You go up this road to the second traffic light. Turn right, drive along Orchard Road, go
5   over the bridge, and the university's on your left.

DRIVER: Go up to the second traffic light, turn right, go across the river, and the university's on my left.

STUDENT: That's right! Look, I'm also going there. Do you mind if I go with you?

10   DRIVER: No, not at all. What are you studying?

STUDENT: Chemistry. It's my first day today.

DRIVER: Are you excited?

STUDENT: No, I'm worried. My first class is with the "Ogre."

DRIVER: And who's the "Ogre"?

15   STUDENT: The new math professor.* They say he's terrible.

DRIVER: Oh, really? What's his name?

STUDENT: I forget.

DRIVER: Peter West?

STUDENT: Yes, that's right. Do you know him?

20   DRIVER: Yes. I'm Peter West.

STUDENT: Oh, no!

———
*Professor = teacher at a university.

(library)

(museum)

(traffic light)

(bus stop)

(corner)

(subway)

(university)

(church)

(supermarket)

(jail)

(parking lot)

(laundry)

(real estate agency)

(barber shop)

(jeweler)

(driver)

(hairdresser)

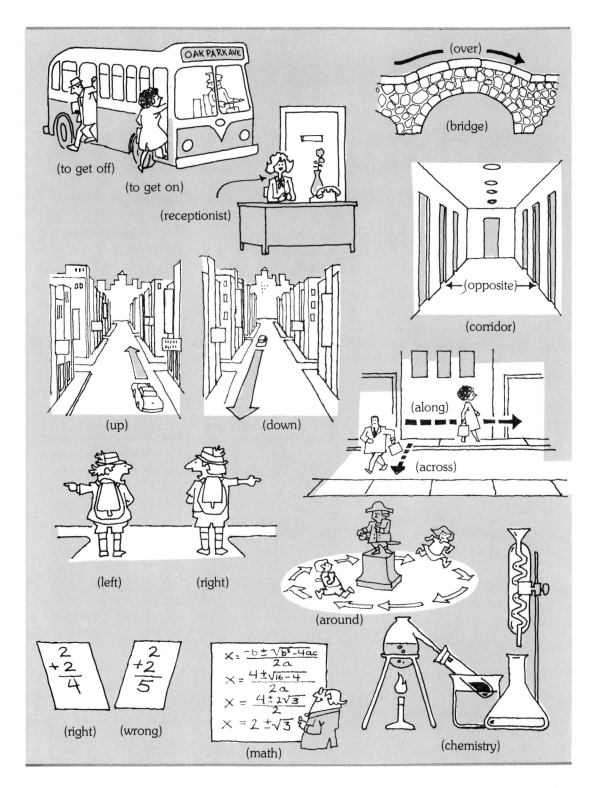

(to get off)

(to get on)

(receptionist)

(over)

(bridge)

(opposite)

(corridor)

(up)

(down)

(along)

(across)

(left)　(right)

(around)

(right)　(wrong)

(math)

(chemistry)

MINI-CONVERSATION 1

A: Which room is the English class in?
B: That's on the fourth floor.
A: Oh, I guess I made a mistake.

MINI-CONVERSATION 2

A: Excuse me, officer. Which bus do I take to the university?
B: Take the number 13 and get off at Church Street.
A: I think I prefer to walk. I never take number 13 buses.

MINI-CONVERSATION 3

A: Excuse me. Is there a laundry near here?
B: Yes. Turn here and there's one just around the corner.

MINI-CONVERSATION 4

A: Excuse me. How do I get to the library?
B: It's up this road, on the corner of Main and Market Streets, opposite the museum.

CONVERSATION PRACTICE

About Conversation 1

1. Who is Mr. Bass looking for? 2. Who told him how to get to Mr. Williams's office? 3. Did he go to the right office? 4. Where does Jack Williams work? 5. Do people often make this mistake?

About Conversation 2

1. What does the driver want to know? 2. Where's the student going? 3. What's he studying at the university? 4. What are you studying at school / the university? 5. Why is the student worried? 6. Who's the "Ogre"? 7. What's he like? 8. Is he new at the university?

Situation 1

Use Cue Book Chart 3. Practice with a friend. You are at the subway on Market Street. You want to go to the fish market.

Situation 2

Use Cue Book Chart 3. You are outside the jail in your car. You want to go to the university.

Situation 3

Use Cue Book Chart 3. You are in the laundry. You want to go to the post office.

SUMMARY OF NEW WORDS

VERBS: REGULAR

to look for / looked for   to turn / turned

VERBS: IRREGULAR

to get on (off) / got on (off)   to tell / told

NOUNS

barber shop(s)	driver(s)	math / mathematics	right
bridge(s)	floor(s)	mistake(s)	road(s)
bus stop(s)	hairdresser(s)	museum(s)	subway(s)
chemistry	jail(s)	parking lot(s)	supermarket(s)
church(es)	jeweler(s)	professor(s)	traffic light(s)
class(es)	laundry (laundries)	real estate agency	university (universities)
corner(s)	left	(agencies)	
corridor(s)	library (libraries)	receptionist(s)	

ADJECTIVES / ADVERBS

left   right   wrong

PREPOSITIONS

across   along   down   opposite   over   up

PHRASES AND EXPRESSIONS

to be right / wrong	Do you mind if . . . ?	Sure.
Could you tell me / us	to make a mistake	to take a / the bus (subway, plane, etc.)

EXERCISES

A. Ask and answer. Use Cue Book Chart 3. Start with **16.**

> STUDENT A: Could you tell me where the theater is?
> STUDENT B: Yes, it's on President Street opposite the drugstore.
>   (*or:* next to the church; behind the restaurant).

17, 18, 19, 20, 21, 22, 23, 24, 25, 26, 27, 28, 29, 30, 31.

B. Ask and answer. Use Cue Book Chart 3. Start with **2** / *around the corner.*

> STUDENT A: Is there a barber shop near here?
> STUDENT B: Yes, there's one around the corner.

1. **3** / behind the barber shop
2. **4** / next to the post office
3. **5** / on the corner of Market Street and Old Willow Road
4. **6** / down near the river
5. **7** / on Old Willow Road
6. **8** / opposite the church
7. **9** / along this street to your left
8. **10** / over there on the corner
9. **11** / next to the hotel
10. **12** / on President Street
11. **14** / across the street
12. **15** / behind the library
13. **16** / on the corner of Main and President Streets
14. **17** / just up the street
15. **18** / opposite the park
16. **19** / near the university
17. **20** / across the bridge
18. **22** / just around the corner
19. **23** / on Orchard Road next to the bank
20. **24** / near the museum
21. **25** / over there on the corner
22. **26** / around the corner to your right
23. **27** / up this street to your left

Grammar Summary

Polite Requests / Embedded Questions

You know these questions: *Where's the office? Who are those people? What time is it? Why do you want these? How old are you?*

The phrase *Could you = Please. Could you tell me / us* and *May I / we ask = Please tell me / us.* Note the word order:

Could you tell me / us May I / we ask	where the office is? who those people are? what time it is? why you want these? which one you prefer? when the party is? how old he is?

NOTE: A simple question *(Is she right? Did I make any mistakes?)* → *Could you tell me **if** she's right? May I ask **if** I made any mistakes?*

DEVELOPING YOUR SKILLS

A. Use "Could you tell me" or "May I ask."

1. Where do you live?	5. When is he getting off the bus?	9. Who used my soap?
2. What does she do?	6. Why are we turning left?	10. When did he come?
3. How are you?	7. Is he looking for something?	11. Where did you buy that?
4. Which one is it?	8. What's the weather like?	12. Were you there?

B. Use the correct preposition.

1. The chemistry student lives *(on / at / near)* the sixth floor.
2. The jeweler has a store *(at / opposite / in)* the drugstore.
3. Could you tell me the way *(along / to / for)* the museum?
4. Mr. Williams's office isn't *(at / along / near)* this corridor. It's *(at / around / in)* the corner next to mine.
5. I'm telling you it isn't in front of the bank. It's *(across / up / behind)* the bank.
6. Don't walk *(in / around / opposite)* the road. A car's coming!
7. The plane flew *(up / over / behind)* the city.
8. I don't want to walk *(over / up / across)* the stairs. I'm too tired.

Talk About Yourself

1. Do you often make mistakes? What kind? What do you do when you make a mistake?
2. When did you last make a mistake?   3. Is there a subway in your town? Is there a library? a museum? a university? Where are they?   4. Tell a friend how to get to your house / apartment: What bus or subway to take. Where to get on. Where to get off. When your friend gets off, how to get to your house / apartment.

Test Yourself

Choose the right word or expression. (1 point each)

1. Could you tell me *(where is the barber shop / where the barber shop is)?*
2. I'm afraid I made a mistake. I took the *(right / left / wrong)* bus.
3. Do you mind if I walk with you? *(Here you are. / Not at all.)*
4. May I ask where the park is? Yes, it's *(down / over / up)* the bridge.
5. Where's the jail? It's *(opposite / across / over)* the street.
6. Could you tell us *(where's the supermarket / where the supermarket is)?*
7. *(May I ask / Do you mind)* if you smoke?
8. My office is on the fifth *(corridor / floor)*, *(along / opposite)* the receptionist.
9. Where's the car? It's in the *(church / parking lot / subway)*.

Total Score _____

What to say . . .

LESSON 6

CONVERSATION

REPORTER:	Now, Rex, what are your plans for the future?
REX KING:	Well, I'm going to make a new movie here at the studio and I'm going to get married.
REPORTER:	That's wonderful news! Who's the lucky girl?
5 REX KING:	Lydia Russell. She was in my last movie.
REPORTER:	And when's the wedding?
REX KING:	We aren't sure yet. Maybe in July.
REPORTER:	Are you getting married here in L.A.?*
REX KING:	Yes, we are.
10 REPORTER:	Could you tell us something about the wedding?
REX KING:	Sure. My new movie's going to be about the wedding.
REPORTER:	That's very interesting.
REX KING:	Yeah! I'm going to call it *The Wedding of the Century*. You see, the guests are going to be
15	the actors. I'm going to have twelve cameras in different places.
REPORTER:	How many guests are you going to have?
REX KING:	Over five hundred. Lydia and I . . .
REPORTER:	The bride and groom . . .
20 REX KING:	Right! We're going to arrive in an open car. Behind us there are going to be five cars with the best man and the ushers and bridesmaids. Also a truck with the band. All the guests
25	are going to be along the street. Everybody's going to wear old-fashioned clothes. It's going to be fantastic!
REPORTER:	I'm sure it is. I guess you're going to have a beautiful reception and a wedding cake.
REX KING:	Sure we are. We're going to have an enormous
30	cake about five meters high. It's going to have stairs and we're going to stand on top of it for photographs.
REPORTER:	Where are you planning to go on your honeymoon?
REX KING:	Oh, I'm not going to tell you that. That's a surprise.

*L.A. = Los Angeles.

New Words

(open) (closed)

(best man)

(old-fashioned) (modern)

(to find)

(movie / TV studio)

(on top (of))

(ushers) (groom) (bridesmaids)

(bride)

(wedding cake)

(guests)

(wedding)

(reception)

20 meters

20 meters

(total area = 400 square meters)

(band)

(truck)

30 meters

(30 meters high)

MINI-CONVERSATION 1

A: Everybody loves your new house.
B: Yes, it's in a beautiful area.
A: You're lucky. How big is it?
B: It's over 250 square meters.
A: I hope you're enjoying the place.
B: Oh, sure. But sometimes it's a little boring, I'm afraid.

MINI-CONVERSATION 2

A: What's in that enormous box?
B: It's a surprise.
A: Are you sure?
B: Sure! I'm going to give it to you on our honeymoon.
A: Fantastic!

MINI-CONVERSATION 3

A: Are you going to finish at the university this year?
B: I hope so.
A: Do you intend to start work immediately?
B: No, I don't think so. I'm planning to take a vacation first.
A: What are your plans for the future? Are you going to stay here?
B: Maybe. I hope to find a job here.
A: And are your parents coming to live with you?
B: I don't know yet, but I really hope not. I plan to get married next year.

CONVERSATION PRACTICE

About the Conversation

1. What does Rex plan to do?   2. What's the wonderful news?   3. Who's his girlfriend?
4. Where's he going to get married?   5. What's the movie going to be about?   6. Who are
the guests going to be?   7. How are the bride and groom going to arrive?   8. Where are the
guests going to stand?   9. What are they going to wear?   10. Where are Rex and Lydia going
to stand for photographs?   11. Where are they going on their honeymoon?

Situation 1

You and a friend are going to make a movie and you are talking about it.

What are you going to call it? (use *Let's*)
What is it going to be like?
Is it going to be in black and white or in color?
Where are you going to make it?

Who's going to be in it?
You and your friend tell the story. (use *going
to*)

Situation 2

You went to an enormous wedding last Saturday. You and a friend are talking about it.

Where was it? What time?
How many people were there?
How many ushers and bridesmaids were
   there?

Talk about the reception.
What did you eat and drink?
Did everybody have a good time? Or was
   there maybe some trouble?

SUMMARY OF NEW WORDS

VERBS: REGULAR

to hope / hoped   to plan / planned*
to intend / intended

VERBS: IRREGULAR

to find / found   to get married / got married

NOUNS

area(s)	bride(s)	groom(s)	meter(s)	surprise(s)	usher(s)
band(s)	bridesmaid(s)	guest(s)	reception(s)	truck(s)	wedding(s)
best man	future	honeymoon(s)	studio(s)		

ADJECTIVES   PREPOSITIONS

| boring | enormous | high | old-fashioned | square | total | on top (of) |
| closed | fantastic | lucky | open | sure | | |

PRONOUNS   ADVERBS   PHRASES AND EXPRESSIONS

everybody   a little   maybe   yet   I hope / think / guess so.   I don't think so.
                                                     I hope / guess not.   to take a vacation

---

*To plan→pla**nn**ing.

EXERCISES

A. Ask and answer. Use Cue Book Chart 3. Start with *you* (sing.) / **30** / *leave my car there.*

    STUDENT A: What are you planning to do at the garage?
    STUDENT B: I intend to leave my car there.

1. you *(pl.)* / **31** / buy some fresh fish
2. Mrs. Bass / **32** / look for her luggage
3. the bridesmaids / **1** / help the bride
4. Mr. Panos / **3** / mail some post cards
5. Ms. Tanaka / **4** / look for her keys
6. Miss Rodriguez / **6** / swim all afternoon
7. everybody / **7** / play tennis
8. you *(sing.)* / **8** / buy some food for the reception
9. the groom / **9** / buy some magazines
10. Pierre / **10** / wait for the number 11 bus
11. Mr. and Mrs. Ahmed / **11** / buy a new watch for their son
12. Alexandra / **12** / buy some shoes for her honeymoon
13. Rex / **13** / make a fantastic new movie
14. you *(pl.)* / **17** / get married
15. the pharmacist / **18** / rent a furnished apartment
16. the children / **19** / look at all the animals
17. the interviewer / **20** / talk to the president
18. you *(sing.)* / **21** / turn left
19. the best man / **22** / cash a check for the groom
20. those little boys / **24** / find a book about snakes

B. Ask and answer. Use Cue Book Chart 1. Start with **1** / *the professor about your test* / *(−)think* or: *(−)guess.*

    STUDENT A: Are you going to argue with the professor about your test?
    STUDENT B: No, I don't think so. *or:* No, I guess not.

1. **2** / with the bride after the wedding / (+)hope
2. **3** / red wine / (+)think
3. **4** / your truck to the reception / (−)think
4. **5** / some wedding cake / (+)hope
5. **6** / on top of the bridge / (+)think
6. **7** / that boring music / (−)hope
7. **8** / some candy for everybody / (+)guess
8. **9** / cards with your guests / (−)think
9. **10** / with the band at your brother's wedding / (+)think
10. **11** / on top of that table / (−)hope
11. **12** / at home tonight / (+)guess
12. **13** / in the corridor / (−)guess

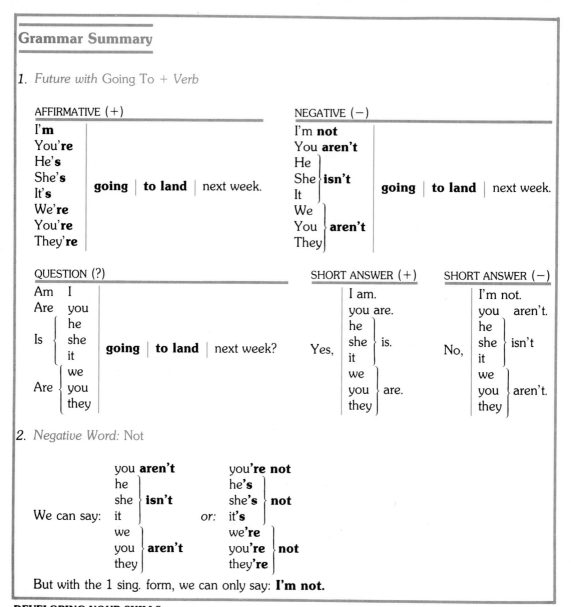

Grammar Summary

1. Future with Going To + Verb

AFFIRMATIVE (+)

I'm
You're
He's
She's
It's **going | to land |** next week.
We're
You're
They're

NEGATIVE (−)

I'm **not**
You **aren't**
He
She **isn't**
It **going | to land |** next week.
We
You **aren't**
They

QUESTION (?)

Am I
Are you
Is he
she
it **going | to land |** next week?
we
Are you
they

SHORT ANSWER (+)

I am.
you are.
he
Yes, she is.
it
we
you are.
they

SHORT ANSWER (−)

I'm not.
you aren't.
he
No, she isn't
it
we
you aren't.
they

2. Negative Word: Not

We can say:
you **aren't**
he
she **isn't**
it
we
you **aren't**
they

or:
you're **not**
he's
she's **not**
it's
we're
you're **not**
they're

But with the 1 sing. form, we can only say: **I'm not.**

DEVELOPING YOUR SKILLS

Complete the sentences.

You don't intend to turn right? (then / not / drive over the bridge)
If you don't intend to turn right, then you're not going to drive over the bridge.

1. The truck driver found his keys? (then / drive home)
2. You don't enjoy old-fashioned things? (then / not / like this museum)
3. The bride and groom left the reception? (then / go on their honeymoon)
4. The box is still open? (then / not / be a surprise)
5. You study a lot? (not / make any mistakes)

6. The total area is over 500 square meters? (be enormous)
7. He isn't looking at the number? (I'm afraid / not / get on the right bus)
8. The guests aren't here yet? (maybe / not / come)
9. I'm lucky? (forget all my troubles)
10. She's talking to her travel agent? (then / maybe / go on a cruise)
11. Everybody's still at the studio? (I guess / make some new TV shows)

Reading

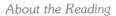

We're planning to open a new factory in São Paulo next year. It's going to be enormous. The total area is going to be 760,000 square meters and the building area is going to be about 250,000. We're going to make trucks and buses. At first we're going to have only about 800
5   people, but in the future we plan to have over a thousand. We intend to make over ten thousand trucks and five thousand buses every year. We hope to sell our products to over a hundred countries.

About the Reading

Ask Mr. Olsen: 1. when they are planning to open the factory. 2. where it is going to be. 3. about the size of the factory. 4. what they are going to make. 5. how many people are going to work there. 6. if they intend to sell only in Brazil.

My name is Sophia. I'm looking for a new job. I have one now, but it's really very boring. I don't like to do the same thing every day. I know somewhere there are many interesting jobs. I hope to find one in the next month or two. I'd like to travel, meet people, and enjoy my work. Sure, nowadays many people stay in one job for many years, but they 5 never really enjoy it. I'm different. Long hours are fine. I enjoy work at night too—when I like the work. I'm sure there are good jobs and I really want to do something interesting.

About the Reading

1. Does Sophia intend to stay in the same job? 2. What does she think of her job? 3. What do you think she does? 4. What boring jobs do you know? 5. Do you enjoy your job? 6. What do you do? 7. What kind of job do you think Sophia is going to like?

Writing

Write about your plans for the future.

Talk About Yourself

1. Are you married? / Are you going to get married or do you hope to get married? 2. How old were you when you got married? / How old would you like to be when you get married? 3. What was your wedding like? / What's your wedding going to be like? 4. Where did you go on your honeymoon? / Where would you like to go on your honeymoon? 5. Talk about weddings in your country.

Test Yourself

Complete the dialogues with the following words. (1 point each)

area   band   boring   high   lucky   maybe   old-fashioned   on top of   so   yet

1. A: What was the ____ like last night?
   B: They played very well.
2. A: What would you like to eat?
   B: I'm not sure ____. ____ some broiled shrimp in butter sauce.
3. A: How ____ is the Eiffel Tower in Paris?
   B: I think it's over 300 meters.
4. A: I got 5,000 Q from the guests at my wedding.
   B: You're ____!
5. A: Are Mr. and Mrs. Jones going to the Bahamas this year?
   B: I don't think ____.
6. A: They're going to open a restaurant ____ that tall building.
   B: That's interesting.
7. A: What's the total ____ of an Olympic swimming pool?
   B: I don't know.
8. A: Do you enjoy ____ things?
   B: No, I don't. I usually find them very ____.

Total Score _____

What to say . . .

Song   I'M GOING TO BE FREE

G
I'm going to take a bus
       C   G
I'm going to leave this lonely town

I'm going to find a place
           C   F   D
Where you and I can settle down
              C
5 We're going to feel the sun

We're going to be so free
          C
I'm going to write a song

About you and me
           G
We're going to walk along
                  Am   D
10 The sandy beach beside the sea.

   Am   D
I don't intend to work my life away
G   Em
I don't intend to listen to what people say
   Am   C   G
I don't intend to fight for money every day
  Am   D
I just intend to be what I want to be
     G   Em
15 I'm never going to work in a noisy factory
   Am   C   D
With people all around to watch and worry me.

      G   C   G
I'm going to bury all my troubles in the sand

You're going to know my hopes
             C   F   D
You're going to be my only friend
            G
20 I'm going to stay with you all night and day
              C
I'm going to think of pretty things I'm going

  to say
          G
I'm going to kiss your lips
                Am   D
I'm going to wipe your tears away.

  Am   D
I don't intend to work from nine to five
G   Em
I don't intend to wait for the future to arrive   25
   Am   C   G
Tomorrow is too late to find that we're alive
      Am   D
We're going to have a home and a family
       G   Em
We're going to be happy in our house by

  the sea
        Am   C
We're going to live together, darling, you
         G
  and me.

LESSON 7

CONVERSATION 1

PETER JACKSON:	Good morning. My name is Peter Jackson. I have an appointment with Mr. Lawson.
RECEPTIONIST:	Mr. Lawson's expecting you. Go right in.*

● ● ●

MR. LAWSON:	Hello, Jackson. Good to see you. Please sit down.
PETER JACKSON:	Thank you.
MR. LAWSON:	Now what can we do for you?
5 PETER JACKSON:	I'd like to apply for a job.
MR. LAWSON:	You used to work for Pro-Gress, right?
PETER JACKSON:	Yes, I used to, but I don't anymore.
MR. LAWSON:	Why did you leave the company?
PETER JACKSON:	Because they didn't pay me enough.
10 MR. LAWSON:	I see. And why are you leaving your present job?
PETER JACKSON:	Because I'm still not earning enough.
MR. LAWSON:	Well, salaries in this business are low, Jackson. But fill out this application
15	form. Maybe we have something for you.

CONVERSATION 2

PERSONNEL MANAGER:	How many words a minute can you type?
MRS. SINCLAIR:	About eighty.
PERSONNEL MANAGER:	That's very good. You can speak German and French well and you can read and
5	understand some Spanish. Is that right?
MRS. SINCLAIR:	Yes, I used to live in Germany before I got married.
PERSONNEL MANAGER:	Can you take shorthand in German and French?
MRS. SINCLAIR:	Yes, I can.
10 PERSONNEL MANAGER:	And can you travel? You see, sometimes we need someone to go to Europe for us.
MRS. SINCLAIR:	Oh! I'd love that.
PERSONNEL MANAGER:	When do you think you can start?
MRS. SINCLAIR:	Immediately! How about today?

*Here, *right* = *immediately*.

(careless) / (careful)

(quick / fast) (slow)

(noisy) (quiet)

(loud) / (soft)

(high)

(low)

(badly) / (well)

(Germany)

(happily) / (sadly)

(child) / (children)

(shorthand)

Do you speak English? Yes, I do.

(to pay)

(to ask (a question)) (to answer (a question)) (to type)

(to fill out (a form / an application))

MINI-CONVERSATION 1

A: I have an appointment with the personnel manager.
B: One minute, please. . . . Mrs. Jones, someone is here to see you.
C: Fine. Send him right in.

MINI-CONVERSATION 2

A: Hello. What can I do for you?
B: I'd like to apply for a job with your company.
A: Please sit down. Can you type?
B: Yes, I can. About 75 words a minute.
A: And do you take shorthand?
B: Well, I used to. I'm sure I can still do it. I'm a hard worker.
A: And how much do you expect to earn?
B: My present salary is low—only 2,000 Q a month. I'd like 2,500.
A: I can understand that. But you know this business doesn't pay very high salaries.

MINI-CONVERSATION 3

A: Hi. Good to see you. How did the band play last night?
B: Very badly. The music was too loud and the place was terribly noisy. I just can't enjoy that kind of evening.

MINI-CONVERSATION 4

A: Does Pablo still sing so loudly?
B: I didn't know he could sing.
A: Oh, yes. He used to sing and play the guitar.
B: I guess you didn't enjoy it, right?
A: No, but what could we do? He lived with us.

CONVERSATION PRACTICE

About Conversation 1

1. What does Peter have?   2. Who is expecting him?   3. What does Peter want?   4. What company did he use to work at?   5. Why did he leave?   6. Why does he want to leave his present job?   7. Are salaries high in his job?   8. What is he going to fill out?

About Conversation 2

1. How many words a minute can Mrs. Sinclair type?   2. What languages can she speak?
3. How does she speak them?   4. Can she understand Spanish?   5. Where did she use to live? When?   6. Can she take shorthand?   7. Can she travel?   8. When can she start?

Situation 1

You are looking for a job and are talking to the personnel manager. He/she wants to know:

    if you can type and how many words a minute
    if you can take shorthand

Situation 2

You applied for a job and are talking to the person you are going to work for if you get the job. He/She asks:

    what kind of job you are looking for
    what you can do

how many languages you can speak and
   which ones
why you are leaving your present job
how much you are earning now and how
   much you'd like to earn
why you would like this job

if you speak English
what schools you went to
where you worked before
what you did there
how much you earned
if you would like to fill out an application

SUMMARY OF NEW WORDS

VERBS: REGULAR

to answer / answered	to ask/asked	to expect / expected	to type / typed
to apply (for) / applied (for)	to earn / earned	to fill out / filled out	

VERBS: IRREGULAR

AUXILIARY VERBS

to pay / paid   to understand / understood   can / could   use(d) to
to sit down / sat down

NOUNS

answer(s)	business(es)	German	personnel	shorthand
application(s)	company (companies)	Germany	question(s)	word(s)
appointment(s)	form(s)	manager(s)	salary (salaries)	worker(s)

ADJECTIVES

PRONOUNS

careful	fast	immediate	low	present	slow	someone	
careless	hard	loud	noisy	quick	soft		

ADVERBS

ADVERBS OF DEGREE

anymore	carelessly	loudly	quietly	softly	so
badly	fast	noisily	sadly	terribly	
carefully	happily	quickly	slowly	well	

PHRASES AND EXPRESSIONS

to come / go right in   Good to see you   to take shorthand   What can I / we do for you?

EXERCISES

A. Ask and answer. Use Cue Book Chart 1. Start with *you* (sing.) / **20** / *Chinese.*

STUDENT A: Can you write Chinese?
STUDENT B: (+) Yes, I can. *or:* (−) No, I can't.

1. you *(sing.)* / **2** / well (−)
2. the manager / **4** / today (+)
3. you *(pl.)* / **5** / with chopsticks (−)
4. we / **8** / plane tickets / here (+)
5. Dimitri and Ali / **9** / chess well (−)
6. Ms. Melody / **10** / softly (+)
7. you *(sing.)* / **12** / on a bus (+)
8. I / **13** / in the corridor (−)
9. the personnel manager / **14** / Spanish (−)
10. you *(sing.)* / **15** / on your head (−)
11. Mrs. Masaki / **18** / to the bus stop (+)
12. the secretaries / **19** / next Saturday (−)

B. Ask and answer. Use Cue Book Chart 4. Start with *Jack Kick* / *play* / *very* / **6** / **7**.

> STUDENT A: How does Jack Kick play?
> STUDENT B: Very well.
> STUDENT C: I don't think so. I think he usually plays badly.

1. Ms. Melody / sing / very / **8** / **9**
2. the children / do their work / **10** / **11**
3. Mr. Grump / work / **12** / **13**

4. Mr. Flap / fly / very / **1** / **2**
5. the manager / work / **3** / **4**
6. Mrs. Chase / drive her taxi / **4** / **5**

C. Ask and answer. Use Cue Book Chart 3. Start with *that announcer* / *work* / **13**.

> STUDENT A: Didn't that announcer use to work in the TV (*or:* movie) studio?
> STUDENT B: Yes, he used to, but he doesn't anymore.

1. you *(sing.)* / live near / **14**
2. she / catch the bus opposite / **15**
3. Ms. Payne / earn a good salary in / **16**
4. Mr. Cook / work at / **17**
5. that clerk / type for / **18**
6. you *(pl.)* / live on / **19**

7. Professor Smith / teach at / **20**
8. Molly / pick up her child near / **21**
9. you *(sing.)* / be a receptionist at / **22**
10. Alexandra and Kiku / be cooks at / **23**
11. Maria / take shorthand at / **24**
12. Raul / expect a lot of children at / **25**

Grammar Summary

1. Modal Verb: Can / Could

AFFIRMATIVE (+)

Now Then	I you he she it we you they	**can** **could**	fly.

NEGATIVE (−)

Now Then	I you he she it we you they	**can't** *(can + not)* **couldn't** *(could + not)*	fly	anymore.

QUESTION (?)

Can **Could**	I you he she it we you they	fly	now? then?

SHORT ANSWER (+)

Yes,	I you he she it we you they	**can.** **could.**

SHORT ANSWER (−)

No,	I you he she it we you they	**can't.** **couldn't.**

2. *Past Tense Auxiliary Verb:* Use(d) To

AFFIRMATIVE (+)

I You He She It We You They	**used**	to fly.

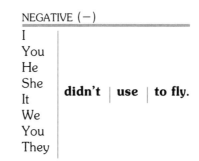

NEGATIVE (−)

I You He She It We You They	**didn't**	**use**	to fly.

QUESTION (?)

Did	I you he she it we you they	**use**	to fly?

SHORT ANSWER(+)

Yes,	I you he she it we you they	**did.** **used to.**

SHORT ANSWER (−)

No,	I you he she it we you they	**didn't.** **didn't use to.**

3. *Adjectives / Adverbs*

Note how we form most adverbs:

bad	→ bad**ly**	He's a bad driver; he drives badly.
careful	→ careful**ly**	She's a careful pilot; she flies carefully.
careless	→ careless**ly**	You're careless; you type carelessly.
happy	→ happ**ily**	They're happy children; they always play happily.
immediate	→ immediate**ly**	I need an immediate answer; answer immediately.
loud	→ loud**ly**	He's a loud man; he always talks loudly.
noisy	→ nois**ily**	That's a noisy plane; it lands so noisily.
quick	→ quick**ly**	He's a quick mechanic; he works quickly.
quiet	→ quiet**ly**	She's a quiet girl; she speaks very quietly.
sad	→ sad**ly**	Why are you so sad? You're walking very sadly.
slow	→ slow**ly**	I'm a slow worker; I usually work slowly.
soft	→ soft**ly**	I like soft music, when the band plays softly.
terrible	→ terri**bly**	That music is terrible; he sings terribly.

NOTE: Adjectives ending in -y change to -i- *(happily, noisily).* Adjectives ending in -le drop the e *(terribly).*

IRREGULAR

fast	→ **fast**	You're a fast driver; you drive too fast.
good	→ **well**	They're good tennis players; they play tennis well.
hard	→ **hard**	She's a hard worker; she works so hard.

DEVELOPING YOUR SKILLS

A. Use the correct adjective or adverb.

1. Please fill out this form *(carefully / careful)*.
2. Our jeweler is a *(careless / carelessly)* driver.
3. That reporter writes very *(bad / badly)*.
4. He used to be a *(fast / quickly)* worker, but he isn't anymore.
5. Did her son use to go to the barber shop *(happy / happily)*? Mine just hated it.
6. The professor spoke *(loud / loudly)* because there were so many people there.
7. The doctor couldn't come *(immediate / immediately)* because he had trouble with his car.
8. Did your company's receptionist use to speak *(good / well)* English?
9. He used to be in the office for only an hour or two every day. He worked very *(slowly / fast)*.
10. I can't live on the first floor. The cars and buses are too *(noisy / noisily)*.
11. The groom waited for two hours, but the bride didn't come. He was very *(sad / sadly)*.
12. Can you please speak *(slow / slowly)*? I'm afraid I can't understand you.
13. We love to listen to his music. He plays so *(soft / softly)*.
14. Our house was always so *(quiet / quietly)* when the children were at school.

B. Answer. Use *can't / couldn't* and the cue.

Would you like to dance? (very good) *Yes, but I really can't. I'm afraid I'm not very good.*
Did he like to take shorthand? (fast enough) *Yes, but he really couldn't. I'm afraid he wasn't fast enough.*

1. Would she like to sing? (very happy)
2. Did they like to drive? (careful enough)
3. Did Yoko and you like to fish? (quiet enough)
4. Would you *(sing.)* like to wear this? (tall enough)
5. Would she like to be Miss America? (pretty enough)
6. Did the boys want to finish their work? (quick enough)
7. Would you *(sing.)* like to swim? (too cold)
8. Did she hope to earn a lot of money? (lucky enough)
9. Did your parents want to take a long vacation? (rich enough)
10. Would you *(pl.)* like some pudding for dessert? (very hungry anymore)

C. Answer.

Can you type well? (+) *Well, I used to type well, but I can't anymore.*
Can he sing? (−) *Well, he didn't use to sing, but maybe he can now.*

1. Can they eat fried food? (+)
2. Can she use chopsticks? (−)
3. Can you *(pl.)* board early? (+)
4. Can we check in here? (−)
5. Can they fish in this river? (+)
6. Can he leave before noon? (−)
7. Can they sell things here? (−)
8. Can you *(pl.)* understand German? (+)
9. Can he study in the afternoon? (−)
10. Can she travel in Russia? (+)

Talk About Yourself

1. What company do you work for? What kind of business is it?   2. How many languages can you speak? Which ones?   3. Can you type / take shorthand? How many words a minute?
4. Talk about things you can do and how well you do them. What can't you do?   5. Talk about things you used to do when you were a young boy / girl. (What you used to do at school, what you used to do after school, in the evening, on weekends, etc.)

Test Yourself

Use an appropriate adjective or adverb. (1 point each)

1. My mother's a good cook. She cooks very ____.
2. George can never sing ____ in the bath. He always sings loudly.
3. Mrs. Masaki used to be a very fast worker, but nowadays she works ____.
4. I want to go to a place where the music is ____ and the food is ____.
5. Her boyfriend is a terrible driver. He drives ____.
6. The manager of our company works fifteen hours a day. She works very ____.
7. I didn't know he was in the room. He came in so ____.
8. Please be ____ with that money. There are many thieves in this area.
9. My children are very sick and I want to see the doctor ____.

Total Score _____

What to say . . .

LESSON 8

CONVERSATION

Chris Daily and Monica Wright are talking with Claude Chapel,
a famous reporter, about his life.

CHRIS: Someone said you were born in Jakarta. Is that right?

CLAUDE: Yes, on April 1,* 1920. My parents worked in a hospital there.

MONICA: But you didn't live in Indonesia very long, did you?

CLAUDE: No. My parents died when I was six and I
5   went to live in Paris with an uncle. I started primary school the following year.

CHRIS: The La Rochelle School, wasn't it?

CLAUDE: No, no, that was the second. First I was at the
Montparnasse, but I hated it. Our teacher used to
10   hit us a lot and I was always in trouble.

MONICA: You went to high school in Munich, didn't you?

CLAUDE: Yes. When I was fourteen, Uncle George got a very good
job with a company in Munich, so we went to live there.
And I got my first job too. I worked for a travel agent.
15   I used to look after the French tourists.

CHRIS: I guess that was terribly exciting for a young boy,
wasn't it?

CLAUDE: No, it became very boring. Always the same places and
the same story all the time: "Ladies and gentlemen, on
20   your right you can see this or that church, and the famous
writer, Mr. X, was born over here in this house." So I left
and went to work for a newspaper. Then the war came in
'39 and I became a reporter.

CHRIS: You were in Russia, weren't you?

25 CLAUDE: Yes, I was. I learned to speak Russian, you know.
I could type it too—and very fast.

MONICA: You can still speak it, can't you?

CLAUDE: No, I'm afraid I can't say anything in Russian anymore.
But I'm boring you, aren't I? I don't . . .

30 MONICA: Oh, no, not at all!

CHRIS: Your life is so interesting!

---

*In dates we say the ordinal number: April first (second, third, etc.).

New Words

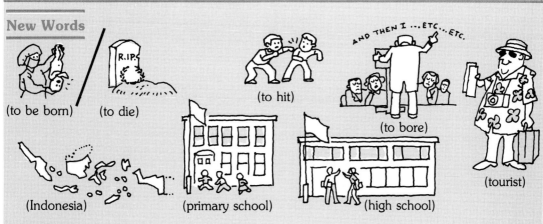

(to be born) / (to die)

(to hit)

AND THEN I ...ETC...ETC.

(to bore)

(tourist)

(Indonesia)

(primary school)

(high school)

DEFINITIONS

aunt: your father's sister or your mother's sister; your uncle's wife.

to become: to start to be: *I was a travel agent, then I became a reporter.*

famous: when a lot of people know about you: *John Lennon was very famous.*

following: next; something that is after something else.

to get a job: to find a job and start to work.

to learn: to study and then to know something.

life: from the time you are born to when you die: *John Lennon had a short, but very exciting life.*

long: *(adv.)* for a long time.

to say: to speak; to tell.

so: *(adv. of degree)* very; *(conj.)* because of that.

uncle: your father's brother or your mother's brother; your aunt's husband.

writer: someone whose job is to write.

MINI-CONVERSATION 1

A: Someone told me Ann's going to become a manager in her father's company.

B: She isn't, is she? She's so young. And she still has a lot to learn, doesn't she?

A: She sure does, but I guess her father doesn't think so.

MINI-CONVERSATION 2

A: How did Mike get the job?

B: You know how it is. His aunt is a famous writer, so she got it for him.

CONVERSATION PRACTICE

About the Conversation

1. Where and when was Claude born?   2. How old was he when his parents died?   3. Who did he live with then?   4. How old was he when he started school?   5. How old were you when you started school?   6. What did Claude's teacher at the Montparnasse use to do?
7. Why did the family go to Munich?   8. What was Claude's first job?   9. Why did he leave

the job?   10. What did he do then?   11. When the war started, what language did he learn?   12. Can he still speak it?   13. How old is Claude today?   14. Do you think he's still working? Doing what?

Situation

You are interviewing a famous / interesting / important person. What questions do you ask? A friend can answer your questions.

SUMMARY OF NEW WORDS

<u>VERBS: REGULAR</u>   ADVERBS   ADVERBS OF DEGREE
to bore / bored   to die / died[1]   to learn / learned   long   terribly

<u>VERBS: IRREGULAR</u>
to be born / was (were) born   to become / became   to hit / hit[2]   to say / said

<u>NOUNS</u>
aunt(s)   Indonesia   primary school(s)   uncle(s)
high school(s)   life (lives)   tourist(s)   writer(s)

<u>ADJECTIVES</u>   CONJUNCTIONS   PHRASES AND EXPRESSIONS
famous   following   so   to get a job

EXERCISES

Ask and answer. First study the charts in the Grammar Summary. Then use the adjective or adverb in Cue Book Chart 4. Start with *the band played / 9 / music at the wedding, didn't they?*

STUDENT A: The band played soft music at the wedding, didn't they?
STUDENT B: Yes, they did.

1. the tourists aren't very / **10** / are they?
2. Jane's aunt was very / **11** / wasn't she?
3. you *(pl.)* expect the children to be / **12** / don't you?
4. that famous writer is a / **13** / man, isn't he?
5. our secretary doesn't type / **1** / does she?
6. I'm afraid I'm very / **2** / aren't I?
7. he isn't very / **3** / is he?
8. my uncle died very / **4** / didn't he?
9. we're going to learn very / **5** / aren't we?
10. she didn't fill out the forms very / **6** / did she?
11. the war was very / **7** / for the country, wasn't it?
12. the high school students were terribly / **8** / weren't they?
13. the interviewer spoke very / **9** / didn't he?

---
[1]To die → dying.
[2]To hit → hitting.

Grammar Summary

1. Tag Questions

PRESENT PROGRESSIVE (+)

I'm		aren't {	I?	
You're			you?	
He's		isn't {	he?	
She's	going,		she?	
It's			it?	
We're		aren't {	we?	
You're			you?	
They're			they?	

PRESENT PROGRESSIVE (−)

I'm	not			am	I?
You	aren't			are	you?
He					he?
She	isn't	going,	is {	she?
It					it?
We					we?
You	aren't			are {	you?
They					they?

SIMPLE PRESENT (+)

I	need		don't {	I?
You				you?
He				he?
She	needs	ome,	doesn't {	she?
It				it?
We				we?
You	need		don't {	you?
They				they?

SIMPLE PRESENT (−)

I	don't		do {	I?
You				you?
He				he?
She	doesn't	need any,	does {	she?
It				it?
We				we?
You	don't		do {	you?
They				they?

SIMPLE PAST (+)

I			I?
You			you?
He			he?
She	needed some,	didn't	she?
It			it?
We			we?
You			you?
They			they?

SIMPLE PAST (−)

I			I?
You			you?
He			he?
She	didn't need any,	did	she?
It			it?
We			we?
You			you?
They			they?

CAN / COULD (+)

I				I?
You				you?
He				he?
She	can		can't	she?
It	could	fly,	couldn't	it?
We				we?
You				you?
They				they?

CAN / COULD (−)

I				I?
You				you?
He				he?
She	can't		can	she?
It	couldn't	fly,	could	it?
We				we?
You				you?
They				they?

NOTE: The future with *going to* is the same as the present progressive (*I'm going to eat, aren't I?*, etc.), the past with *used to* is the same as the simple past (*He used to type well, didn't he?*, etc.), and *would* is the same as *could* (*You'd like some dessert, wouldn't you?*, etc.)

PRESENT: TO BE (+)

I'm			aren't {	I?
You're				you?
He's		isn't {		he?
She's	famous,			she?
It's				it?
We're		aren't {		we?
You're				you?
They're				they?

PRESENT: TO BE (−)

I'm	not		am	I?
You	aren't		are	you?
He			is {	he?
She	isn't	famous,		she?
It				it?
We				we?
You	aren't		are {	you?
They				they?

PAST: TO BE (+)

I	was		wasn't	I?
You	were		weren't	you?
He				he?
She	was	right,	wasn't {	she?
It				it?
We				we?
You	were		weren't {	you?
They				they?

PAST: TO BE (−)

I	wasn't		was	I?
You	weren't		were	you?
He				he?
She	wasn't	right,	was {	she?
It				it?
We				we?
You	weren't		were {	you?
They				they?

THERE IS / THERE ARE (+)

There's a manager, isn't there?
There are some managers, aren't there?
There was a manager, wasn't there?
There were some managers, weren't there?

THERE IS / THERE ARE (−)

There isn't a manager, is there?
There aren't any managers, are there?
There wasn't a manager, was there?
There weren't any managers, were there?

2. *The Word* So

So can mean:

very: It's **so** hot, isn't it?

because of that: I listened to the radio **because** I didn't like the TV shows.
        I didn't like the TV shows, **so** I listened to the radio.

yes / no: Is he saying something? I think **so.** (i.e., "Yes, I think he is.") *or:* I don't think **so.**
        (i.e., "No, I don't think he is.")

He's good-looking, isn't he?

I don't think so.

DEVELOPING YOUR SKILLS

A. Say the sentences using the tag question.

She's tall . . . *She's tall, isn't she?*

1. I'm noisy . . .
2. You're quiet . . .
3. He's young . . .
4. She's beautiful . . .
5. It's old . . .
6. She enjoys surprises . . .
7. We intend to apply . . .
8. The workers want good salaries . . .
9. He learns quickly . . .
10. We expect to pay . . .
11. We can go . . .
12. You can get a job . . .
13. They can talk . . .
14. I can learn . . .
15. He can ask . . .

B. Now say the sentences again in the negative: *She isn't tall . . . She isn't tall, is she?*

C. Now say the sentences again in the simple past. Do 1–5 in the negative, 6–10 in the affirmative, 11–15 in the negative: *She wasn't tall . . . She wasn't tall, was she?*

D. Use tag questions to complete the sentences.

1. Nowadays teachers don't normally hit their students, . . . ?
2. Mr. Penn expects to get a job in the new high school, . . . ?
3. There are still some tourists in the museum, . . . ?
4. They couldn't just leave the room, . . . ?
5. You're going to apply for the job, . . . ?
6. The plane took off late, . . . ?
7. There isn't a laundry nearby, . . . ?
8. He didn't find his aunt and uncle, . . . ?
9. They were wrong about Mr. Wise, . . . ?
10. It was a wonderful surprise, . . . ?
11. He's a good friend of yours, . . . ?
12. This seat isn't taken, . . . ?
13. They said they learned a lot, . . . ?
14. She used to be a writer, . . . ?

Reading

It was late Monday night, December 8, 1980. A man and his wife paid the taxi-driver and walked slowly to the large apartment building where they lived. The man walked behind his wife. Someone called "John!" and when the man turned to answer, he was shot.[1]

"Do you know what you just did?" the doorman[2] asked the killer.[3]

5   "I just shot John Lennon," the killer answered.

John Lennon was born in Liverpool, England, on October 9, 1940. When he was only five his father left home and John went to live with an aunt. He studied at Dovedale Primary School, but he always thought it terribly boring. When he was still very young, he used to sing a lot and to write about love. He wanted to become rich and famous.

---

[1]To shoot / shot: 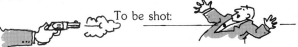 To be shot:

[2]A *doorman* opens the door for people in large apartment buildings.

[3]Killer:

10   John loved music, so one day his mother bought him a guitar. He never studied music, but he learned to play—and very well, too. At school he started his first group,[4] the Quarrymen. Then in 1956 he met Paul McCartney, who was also a fine young musician.[5] Then George Harrison and Ringo Starr came, and in 1962 the Beatles were born.

        They became famous immediately. People—young and old—bought their records. Lennon
15   wrote beautiful music with his friend McCartney. He also wrote books and made movies. In the 1970s,[6] after the Beatles made their last record, Lennon lived quietly with his wife, Yoko, and their young son. But he was still often in the news. He and his wife worked hard for peace.[7]

        When he died, radio stations from New York to Moscow played his music, and they do today. When a good man dies, his work still lives.

Writing

Write about an interesting person you know or about someone famous.

Talk About Yourself

1. Where were you born?   2. What schools did / do you go to? (primary / high /university)
3. What was your first job? What kind of work was it?   4. Talk about your father and mother. Where were they born? What do / did they do?

Test Yourself

Make sentences. (2 points each)

1. left / earn / he / very much / didn't / so / his / job / he
2. really / me / her / bore / stories / long
3. didn't / uncle / manager / became / the personnel / your / he / ?
4. them / didn't / used / her / to hit / father / he / ?
5. nice / she / Mrs. Drake / is / person / a / very / isn't / ?

Total Score _____

What to say . . .

Am I boring you?

---
[4]Group: a small band.
[5]A musician plays music.
[6]1970s: 1970, 1971, 1972 . . . 1979.

[7]Peace:

Song   ABOUT MY FAMILY

A
My parents were in love when they were sixteen
B
They didn't get married and they wore no ring
E   A
My mother at the time was a teenage queen
B   E
And I was born one morning in the following spring.

A
5   My father was a singer in a western band
B
My mother used to dance in a cabaret
E   A
My sister was a movie star, she wasn't very grand
B   E
My brother was a robber and he lived in L.A.

E7   A
You didn't know, did you?
B
10   About my family
E
You were so wrong, weren't you?
A
About my history
You have a friend, don't you?
B
You say he's just like me,
15   So wait a little longer
E
And you're going to see . . .

A
Aunt Mary was the sheriff of a lawless town
B
My cousin was a porter in a cheap hotel
E   A
My uncle was a builder but his houses fell down
B   E
20   His daughter killed a man and she died in the jail.

A
My father left his job in the western band
B
My mother left my father and the cabaret
E   A
My sister found my brother and she joined his gang
B   E
And I am still waiting for the judgment day.

LESSON 9

CONVERSATION 1

OLGA: Were there many people at the Kanes' reception?
JULIA: Yes, there were. There were people everywhere.
OLGA: Who was there?
JULIA: Everybody was there. There was Wilbur Reed . . .
5 OLGA: Wilbur Reed?
JULIA: That crazy millionaire who always brings his cat.
OLGA: Oh! Who else was there?
JULIA: There was Pamela Mitchell, the famous movie star,
and Billy Miles. You remember him.
10 OLGA: I don't think so.
JULIA: Of course you do. He's the one that used to bring
his snake to school.
OLGA: Oh, yes! And one day somebody put it in Miss
Pringle's purse. I remember him now. We used
15 to call him "Snakeman."
JULIA: Ouch!
OLGA: What's the matter, Julia? Why are you walking so
slowly?
JULIA: It's my foot. Tiny stood on it.
20 OLGA: Who's Tiny?
JULIA: That enormous man who's a friend of the Kanes'.
You know—the boxing champion. I'm sure he weighs
over 150 kilos.

CONVERSATION 2

JOHN: Why didn't you come to the political meeting Wednesday?
JACK: I just don't like politics. You know that. And I hate
politicians! But why? Did anything exciting happen?
JOHN: No. But I can't understand you, Jack. You never go
5 anywhere or meet anyone who can help you. So many
important people go to those meetings. A few were
there Wednesday. Even Paul Hope was there.
JACK: Who's Paul Hope?
JOHN: Oh, Jack! You *are* funny! He's just the man who's
10 going to be our next prime minister.

New Words

(to forget) / (to remember)

(million)

(to weigh)

(millionaire)

(with glasses) / (without glasses)

(to win)   (to lose)

(champion)

(movie star)

(boxing)

(foot)   (feet)

(a lot) / (a few)   (politician)   (funny)

MINI-CONVERSATION 1

A: What are you looking for?

B: My glasses. Maybe I'm crazy, but I thought I put them somewhere on this table a few minutes ago. Now I can't find them anywhere. And I can't see anything without them.

A: How do you expect to find them then?

MINI-CONVERSATION 2

A: There's somebody at the door. Please see who it is!

B: There wasn't anybody there.

A: Nobody?

B: No. No one. I think you made a mistake.

MINI-CONVERSATION 3

A: Do you enjoy your house in the country?
B: No, I hate it. Nothing happens. There's nobody to talk to, nothing interesting to do, nowhere exciting to go. It's awful.
A: Yes, in the city there's always somebody to talk to. And there's usually something to do or somewhere to go, isn't there?
C: I don't know. In a big city everyone's too busy. They never talk to anyone else or do anything or go anywhere. And it's dirty everywhere and everything's too noisy.
A: I guess there's nowhere really nice anymore, is there?

MINI-CONVERSATION 4

A: I went out with someone really exciting last night.
B: Anyone I know?
A: Marilyn Thompson.
B: I remember her. Isn't she the girl with glasses who likes politics so much?
A: Yes, we met her at that political meeting last spring. She hopes to be prime minister someday. She's even a fantastic politician *now*. She likes everyone!

CONVERSATION PRACTICE

About Conversation 1

1. Were there many people at the Kanes'?   2. Was Wilbur Reed there?   3. Who is he?
4. Who else was there?   5. What did Billy Miles do when he was a student?   6. What's the matter with Julia's foot?   7. Who's Tiny? Is he very heavy? How much does he weigh?

About Conversation 2

1. Why didn't Jack go to the meeting?   2. Did anything exciting happen?   3. Why does John like political meetings?   4. Were any important people at the meeting Wednesday?   5. Who is Mr. Hope?

Situation 1

You are talking to a reporter about the Kanes' reception.

He / She wants to know how many people were there.
     You tell him / her how many.
He / She asks what you ate and drank.
     Tell him / her.
He / She wants to know who you talked to and what you talked about.
     You tell him / her.
He / She wants to know if you enjoyed the reception.
     You did or you didn't. Tell him / her why.

Situation 2

You lost something and are talking to a receptionist about it.

You lost your . . . . You had a meeting with their manager the day before and you think you left it on his table.
     She wants to know what the thing is like.
You tell her the size, the color, and what kind it is.
     She tells you if / where she found it.

EXERCISES

A. Say. Use Cue Book Chart 4. Start with *There are those men. They drive so / 1.*

There are those men. They drive so carefully.
There are those men who drive so carefully.

1. There's the new architect. He works so / **2**
2. That's the one. She takes shorthand so / **3**
3. Paul Hope's the politician. He talks so / **4**
4. That's the soccer player. He runs so / **5**
5. There's the man. He remembers you so / **6**
6. That's the pilot. He always lands so / **7**
7. There's the woman. She said "Cheers!" so / **8**
8. That's the doctor. She speaks so / **9**
9. Those are the children. They sang so / **10**
10. Jack's the one. He's standing on the corner so / **11**

B. Ask.

That's the agent. He lost his job.
Is that the agent who lost his job? (NOTE: *person* + who)
or: That's the fish. It weighs five kilos.
Is that the fish that weighs five kilos? (NOTE: *thing* + that)

1. That's the woman. She only wears modern clothes.
2. Those are the purses. They are in fashion.
3. That's his uncle. He loves boxing.
4. This is the perfume. It comes from Paris.

---
[1]To put → pu**tt**ing.
[2]To win → wi**nn**ing.

5. That's the one. She's an awful actress.
6. That's the actor. He hopes to be a movie star someday.
7. That's the movie. It's so funny.
8. Those are the children. They remembered my name.
9. This is the child. She was born on a bus.
10. That's the clerk. She won 30,000 Q.
11. These are the women. They planned to fill out the applications.
12. This is the book about politics. It's so exciting.
13. That's the man. He put poison in his wife's food.
14. That's the show. It has the crazy announcer.

Grammar Summary

1. *Pronouns: -body, -one, -thing / Adverbs: -where*

(+)	(+)	(?)	(−)
everybody	somebody	anybody	nobody (*or:* not . . . anybody)
everyone	someone	anyone	no one (*or:* not . . . anyone)
everything	something	anything	nothing (*or:* not . . . anything)
everywhere	somewhere	anywhere	nowhere (*or:* not . . . anywhere)

NOTE: When we use an adjective with these pronouns, the adjective comes after:

I met **an important person.** *but:* I met **someone important.**
I saw **a funny thing.** I saw **something funny.**
I don't know **any interesting stories.** I don't know **anything interesting.**
Let's go to **a nice place.** Let's go **somewhere nice.**

2. *Relative Pronouns: Who / That as Subject*

She's the one. She lost her purse.
She's the one **who / that** lost her purse.

These are the glasses. They're expensive.
These are the glasses **that** are expensive.

NOTE: Relative pronouns are always followed by a 3 sing. or 3 pl. verb: *I'm the one who remembers everything. You're the man who is learning the music, aren't you? We use that for things, but we can use who or that for people.*

3. *Who / What / When / Where / How + Infinitive / Present Progressive*

I (don't) know **who to call.** I (don't) know **who I'm calling.**
I (don't) know **what to do.** I (don't) know **what I'm doing.**
I (don't) know **when to arrive.** I (don't) know **when I'm arriving.**
I (don't) know **where to go.** I (don't) know **where I'm going.**
I (don't) know **how to get** there. I (don't) know **how we're getting** there.

DEVELOPING YOUR SKILLS

A. Use the correct word.

1. There isn't *(something / anything)* good in the fridge.
2. Didn't *(no one / anyone)* lose a knife?
3. *(Everything / Everybody)* enjoyed that funny little man.
4. I'm sorry, but we can't do *(anything / nothing)* this afternoon.
5. I'm not sure where I put it, but I think it was *(everywhere / somewhere)* in the kitchen.
6. There just isn't *(anything / anywhere)* nearby where we can learn to type.
7. I'm afraid *(no one / anyone)* remembers who he is.
8. I hope there's going to be *(everywhere / somewhere)* to sit down. Maybe we can find *(some / any)* chairs before the reception.
9. A few people who came knew *(everything / anything)* about politics.
10. Even the prime minister hoped there was *(something / anything)* exciting to see.

B. Make sentences. Use *don't / doesn't know* + question word + infinitive.

Where can they turn? *They don't know where to turn.*

1. When can she arrive?
2. How can I win?
3. Who can I speak to?
4. What can he say?
5. How can they apply for the job?
6. Where can I get off?
7. What can she bring to the party?
8. Where can he land?
9. Who can I ask?
10. What can we use?

Reading

Student Hits Bull's Eye

Yesterday afternoon there was a political meeting at Liberty Park. There were over 5,000 people, and police officers were everywhere. When the prime minister left his car, Larry Young, a student
5 from Boswell University, gave him a letter. "Can't anyone remember the poor, hungry people? Not even you, Mr. Prime Minister?" Mr. Young said loudly.

Mr. John Bull, a young politician who lives in
10 Boswell and who was with the prime minister, said something quietly to Mr. Young, who then hit him in the eye. The police immediately took Young to the station. The prime minister went in the building without Mr. Bull, who drove with the officers to the
15 police station. Nobody knows yet what was in the letter or what Mr. Bull said to the student. We only know that no one wins and everyone loses when this kind of thing happens.

1. What kind of meeting was there?   2. Where was it?   3. Were there many people there?
How many?   4. Who is Larry Young?   5. Who is John Bull?   6. What did Larry do?
7. What did the police do?   8. What did the prime minister do?   9. Where did Mr. Bull go?
10. What do you think Larry wrote in the letter?   11. What do you think Mr. Bull said to
Larry?   12. Where do you think Larry is now? Why?

Talk About Yourself

1. What's the name of your president / prime minister?   2. Are there many politicians in your
town? Do you know any?   3. Do you like politics? Why?   4. Describe a political meeting or
reception you went to.   5. When was the last time you hit someone (or someone hit you)? Why
did it happen?

Test Yourself

Complete the dialogues with the following words. (1 point each)

anyone   anywhere   everywhere   nowhere   something
anything   everybody   nothing   somebody   somewhere

1. A: But that's very expensive!
   B: ____ is inexpensive nowadays.
2. A: Was there ____ in the house?
   B: I saw no one.
3. A: Where's ____?
   B: They're all downtown.
4. A: What's the matter?
   B: There's ____ in my eye.
5. A: Can I help you?
   B: Yes, I'm looking for ____ to stay.

6. A: Who do you want to take?
   B: ____ who can speak the language.
7. A: Where can I put these bottles?
   B: Just put them ____.
8. A: Was the supermarket very busy?
   B: Oh, yes. There were people ____.
9. A: Do you know ____ about his salary?
   B: No, nothing.
10. A: Where did you go last night?
    B: ____. I stayed home and read.

Total Score _____

What to say . . .

LESSON 10

CONVERSATION 1

MIKE: Hi, Teddy. Did you have an accident?

TEDDY: Yes, it happened while I was working. Someone
broke my finger.

MIKE: What happened?

5   TEDDY: Well, I was going into the bedroom when suddenly
this woman woke up. I tried to run, but it was
too late. Man! I thought she was going to kill me.
Then while I was lying on the ground outside
I looked up and saw the number on the door.

10   It was 13 Edison Avenue.

MIKE: But that's Mrs. Kim's address. She's a karate
champion. I never go to her house.

TEDDY: Well, now I know. Next time I'm going to choose
the people I rob very carefully.

CONVERSATION 2

OFFICER: What can I do for you, ma'am?

LUCILLE: I want to report a robbery.

OFFICER: Your name and address, please.

LUCILLE: Lucille Snob, 35 Weston Drive.

5   OFFICER: Now, can you tell us what happened?

LUCILLE: Someone came into our house while we were asleep and
stole my jewelry. Oh! I hope you can catch him.

OFFICER: Anything else?

LUCILLE: Well, yes. He went into the kitchen and ate

10   a lot of our food.

OFFICER: I guess he was hungry. But how do you know
it was a man?

LUCILLE: Because he left a note and thanked us for the
meal. He signed it "Mike."

New Words

(asleep)

(to break)

(to lie)

(to sit)

(to stand)

(to catch)

(to rob)
(robbery)

(robber)

(accident)

(karate)

(gun)

(arm)

(to kill)

(tooth)
(teeth)

(in)
(inside)
(outside)
(into)
(ground)

(handkerchief)

(wallet)

(finger)
(ring)

(jewel) (jewelry)

(diamond)

(gold)

(nose)
(ear)
(earring)
(mouth)
(neck)
(necklace)

DEFINITIONS

to choose: to look at many things and then take one or two.
  note: short letter.
to sign: to write your name.
to steal: when you rob someone, you steal their things: *Thieves and robbers steal and rob.*
  suddenly: very quickly (usually a surprise).
to thank: to say thank you.
to wake up: not to be asleep anymore.

MINI-CONVERSATION 1

A: Was your house ever robbed?
B: No, never. Was yours?
A: Yes, last night while we were asleep. They stole our clothes, my cassette recorder, and Fernando's camera.

MINI-CONVERSATION 2

A: What were you doing when the accident happened?
B: Pete was trying to kiss me.
A: Were you driving?
B: No. He was.

MINI-CONVERSATION 3

A: Tell us what happened.
B: We were walking down the street when suddenly someone hit me.
A: Did he have a gun?
B: Yes, and he wore a handkerchief over his mouth and nose.
A: What else did he do?
B: He stole my gold watch, our wedding rings, my wife's diamond necklace, and her earrings.
A: Didn't he take your wallet?
B: No, there was nothing in it.

CONVERSATION PRACTICE

About Conversation 1

1. What happened to Teddy? 2. What was Teddy going to do in the bedroom? 3. What's Teddy's job? 4. Who's Mrs. Kim? 5. What did she do to Teddy? 6. What's Mrs. Kim's address? 7. Does Mike ever go to her house? 8. What is Teddy going to do next time?

About Conversation 2

1. What happened at 35 Weston Drive? 2. Who was robbed? 3. What did the thief steal?
4. What were the Snobs doing when he robbed their house? 5. What did the thief do in the kitchen? 6. How do they know it was a man?

Situation 1

A man was robbed in your building. A police officer wants to ask you some questions.

You tell him / her to come in and to sit down.
You ask him / her if he / she would like a cup of coffee.
> He / She doesn't. He / She asks if you know the man who was robbed.
You don't.
> He / She wants to know where you were between 5:00 and 8:00 last evening.
You tell him where you were and what you were doing.

Situation 2

Your house was robbed while you were at the movies. You want to report the robbery.

Give the officer your name and address.
> He / She asks what the thieves stole.
You tell him / her.
> He / She asks if you saw anyone.
A man was leaving when you arrived.
> He / She asks what the man was like.
You tell him what he was like and what he was wearing.
> He / She thanks you and says they're going to try to find the man.

VERBS: REGULAR

to kill / killed   to rob / robbed[1]   to sign / signed   to thank / thanked   to try / tried

VERBS: IRREGULAR

			ADVERBS	
to break / broke	to choose / chose	to steal / stole	ever	outside
to catch / caught	to lie / lay[2]	to wake up / woke up	inside	suddenly

NOUNS

accident(s)	earring(s)	gun(s)	karate	necklace(s)	robber(s)
arm(s)	finger(s)	handkerchief(s)	meal(s)	nose(s)	robbery (robberies)
diamond(s)	gold	jewel(s)	mouth(s)	note(s)	tooth (teeth)
ear(s)	ground	jewelry	neck(s)	ring(s)	wallet(s)

ADJECTIVES	PREPOSITIONS	CONJUNCTIONS	PHRASES AND EXPRESSIONS	
asleep	into	while	Man!	to be robbed

EXERCISES

A. Ask and answer. Use Cue Book Chart 5, the simple past tense, and the correct possessive adjective. Start with *He / to hit / 1.*

> STUDENT A: What happened?
> STUDENT B: He hit his head.

1. I thought / **2** / to be too long
2. She / to lose / **3** / in an accident
3. I / to break / **4** / last night
4. They never / to open / **5** *(pl.)*
5. He / to lose / **6**
6. I / to lie on / **7** / too long
7. They / to forget / **8** *(pl.)*
8. I / to need something for / **9**
9. They / to choose / **10** *(pl.)*
10. I / to try to use / **11** / but I couldn't
11. He / to put / **12** / on the table
12. She / to put the ring on / **13**
13. They / to wear / all / **14** *(pl.)*
14. She / to forget / **15**
15. We / to pick up / **16** *(pl.)*

B. Ask and answer. Use Cue Book Chart 3. Start with *you* (sing.) / **7** / *waiting for a friend.*

> STUDENT A: What were you doing at the park?
> STUDENT B: I was waiting for a friend.

1. Mr. Chen / **8** / weighing the vegetables
2. Mrs. Rodriguez / **9** / using the telephone
3. you *(pl.)* / **11** / choosing our wedding rings
4. Mr. Gunn / **12** / trying to buy a new wallet
5. you *(sing.)* / **13** / applying for a job
6. they / **14** / reporting an accident
7. your aunt / **15** / hoping to see my uncle
8. the girls / **16** / buying tickets for the show
9. the thief / **17** / stealing money
10. your mother / **18** / paying the rent

---

[1] To ro**bb**ing.
[2] To l**ie** → l**y**ing.

Grammar Summary

1. Past Progressive Tense

PRESENT PROGRESSIVE	
I'm	
You're	
He's	
She's	
It's	eating.
We're	
You're	
They're	

PAST PROGRESSIVE		
I	**was**	
You	**were**	
He		
She	**was**	eating.
It		
We		
You	**were**	
They		

2. Conjunctions: When / While

If two things happen at the same time we use *while:*

> Johnny usually sings **while** he's taking a bath.
> Johnny sang **while** he took a bath.
> Johnny was singing **while** he was taking a bath.

If one thing is happening and then a second thing happens, we use *when:*

> Peter talks. Everybody listens. → Everybody listens **when** Peter talks.
> The robber saw the police officer. He ran. → The robber ran **when** he saw the police officer.
> Jack was driving very fast. He had an accident. → Jack was driving very fast **when** he had the accident.

NOTE: We can also start a sentence with *when* or *while:*

> **While** he's taking a bath Johnny usually sings.
> **When** Peter talks everybody listens.

3. Not Using Who / That

We don't need to use *who* or *that* when they refer to the object:

> This is **the man.** I robbed **him.** → This is **the man (who(m) / that)** I robbed.*
> I have **the note.** Teddy signed **it.** → Here's **the note (that)** Teddy signed.

DEVELOPING YOUR SKILLS

A. Say. Use Cue Book Chart 1, the past progressive, and *while.* Start with *They / 1 / you / 2.*

They were arguing while you were dancing.

1. They / (−)**3** / they / **4**
2. The family / **5** / you / **6**

---

*When a person is the object, we sometimes use *whom*, not *who*: *the man whom I robbed.* But normally we say: *the man I robbed.*

3. I / **7** / to the car radio / you / **8** / the food
4. We / **9** / cards / she / **10**
5. I / **11** / quietly in the living room / he / **12**
6. No one / **13** / the professor / **14**
7. They / **15** / outside / he / **16** / to the police officers
8. We / **17** / for the bus / you / **18** / across the street
9. Mother / **19** / I / **20** / to my sister

B. Choose *when* or *while*.

1. I was still asleep *(when / while)* the robbery happened.
2. They were signing the forms *(when / while)* you were waiting for them.
3. He's learning karate *(when / while)* he's in jail.
4. I was walking along the street *(when / while)* somebody stole my wallet.
5. He hit him in the mouth *(when / while)* he caught him.
6. She broke her finger *(when / while)* she tried to pick up the package.
7. I didn't have a gun *(when / while)* I was robbed.
8. They were lying outside *(when / while)* suddenly it became very cold.
9. The children came into the room *(when / while)* I was thanking their parents.
10. He killed the snake *(when / while)* I slept quietly in the chair.

C. What were they doing at 5 o'clock?

1. The young man . . .
2. The old woman . . .
3. The police officer . . .
4. The thief . . .
5. The young girl . . .
6. The taxi-driver . . .
7. The cook . . .
8. The two drivers . . .
9. The dog . . .
10. The boy . . .

Reading

Dear Hector and Lucille:

    I hope you had a great evening. And I hope you don't mind if I used your house while you went dancing. Thanks for the wonderful meal. The chicken was delicious, the wine was great, and the dessert was all right too. (What was it? Some kind of pudding?)

5   *Your suits were a little old-fashioned, Hector, so I didn't take them, but I really liked your dresses, Lucille. Maybe Hector doesn't buy many new clothes because you use all his money. I didn't like your jewelry very much, but I took it because . . . well, gold is gold. I guess you wore all your diamonds tonight, because there weren't any in your jewelry box. And my wife is going to love the perfume! Thanks.*

10
                                                    Yours,

                                                    Mike

P.S. Here's 100 Q. Maybe you can buy something nice the next time you're downtown, Hector. Men need to wear good-looking things too.

About the Reading

1. Where were Hector and Lucille? 2. Who is Mike? 3. Did he enjoy the meal? What did he have? 4. Why didn't Mike take Hector's suits? 5. Why does Mike think Hector doesn't buy many clothes? 6. Did he like Lucille's jewelry? Why did he take it then? 7. Why did Mike leave some money with his letter? 8. What do you think Hector and Lucille are going to do when they arrive home?

Writing

Write a note to a friend thanking him / her for a meal. Use the Reading and the following information to help you:
1. Thank the person.
2. Say he / she cooks very well.
3. Talk about the first course, the main course, and the dessert.
4. Say it was the first time you ever had . . . and you enjoyed it very much.

Talk About Yourself

1. Was your house ever robbed? 2. Are there many robberies in your town? 3. What happens when they catch a thief?

Test Yourself

Complete the paragraph with the following words. Use the past progressive or the simple past. (1 point each)

to choose   to lie   to sign   to try   to walk
to leave   to see   to thank   to wake up   to write

While I ____ in front of the Smiths' house, I ____ an open window. It was very cold outside and I needed some warm clothes, so I went inside. In the bedroom I saw Mr. Smith. He ____ in bed asleep. I ____ to be very quiet. I went to the closet, opened it, and saw an enormous number of clothes. While I ____ a suit, suddenly Mr. Smith ____. I stayed in the closet while he went to the bathroom. Then he came to bed and in a few minutes was asleep. I ____ the closet with two suits over my arm. I went into the living room and put on a jacket. The suit was not in fashion, but it was warm enough. And it was my size too. I ____ a note and ____ Mr. Smith for the suits. Of course I (−) ____ my name. Maybe I'm a thief, but I'm not crazy!

Total Score _____

What to say . . .

Hands up!

I was just looking.

LESSON 11

CONVERSATION 1

PABLO:	Can I use your telephone?
PEPITA:	Sure
PABLO:	*(dials)* The line's busy.[1] *(dials again)* Good. It's ringing now.
5 OPERATOR:	Truman and Fitzgerald. Good morning.
PABLO:	Sales department, please. I'd like to speak to Mr. Sanchez.
OPERATOR:	Hold the line, please.
MR. SANCHEZ:	Juan Sanchez speaking.
10 PABLO:	Hello. Dad, can I borrow your car? Pepita and I are going out tonight and I thought . . .
MR. SANCHEZ:	What! When I was your age we used to walk when we wanted to go somewhere. And besides, you don't even have a driver's license.
15 PABLO:	Pepita does.
MR. SANCHEZ:	Forget it. I'm not going to lend you my car.
PABLO:	*(to Pepita)* He hung up!

CONVERSATION 2

MR. CHEN:	I'd like to cash some traveler's checks. Can I do that here?
CLERK:	Oh, yes. Just sign them, please.
MR. CHEN:	Do you have another pen? Mine doesn't work.[2]
5 CLERK:	Certainly. How would you like the money, sir?
MR. CHEN:	In 20 Q bills. And I'd like some change too.
CLERK:	May I see your passport, please?
MR. CHEN:	Oh, I left it in my other suit.
CLERK:	Well, do you have any other identification?
10 MR. CHEN:	No, I don't have anything with me.
CLERK:	I'm afraid I need to see some identification.
MR. CHEN:	Oh, dear! Well, I have a little Chinese money. Can I exchange it for American money?
CLERK:	Yes, of course. That's not a problem.

---

[1]When someone is talking on the phone, that *line* is *busy.*

[2]He's working: He isn't working: It's working: It isn't working:

New Words

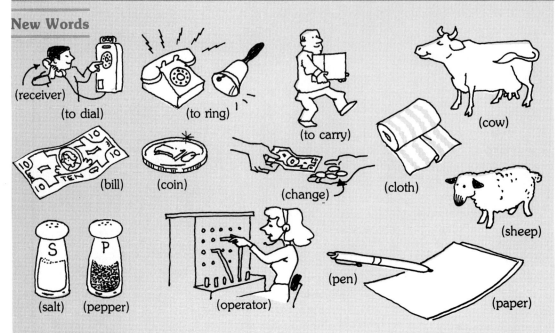

(receiver) (to dial) (to ring) (to carry) (cow)

(bill) (coin) (change) (cloth) (sheep)

(salt) (pepper) (operator) (pen) (paper)

DEFINITIONS

again: a second (third, fourth, etc.) time.

age: how old you are.

to answer the phone: to pick up the receiver and say "Hello" or "X speaking": *When the phone rings we always try to answer it quickly.*

to begin: to start.

call: when you use the phone to call someone, you are *making a call.*

collect call: when the person who gets the call (not the person who is calling) pays.

department: an area in a business office (Personnel Department, Sales Department, etc.), or in a university (Mathematics Department, Chemistry Department, Spanish Department, etc.), or in a store (jewelry department, shoe department, children's department, men's department, etc.).

driver's license: a paper that says you may drive a car: *You can't drive if you don't have a (driver's) license.*

to exchange: to give one thing and get another; you exchange something *for* something else.

foreigner: a person from another country.

to hang up: to put the receiver down on the phone after you finish a call.

to hear: to use your ears: *Do you hear the phone? It's ringing.*

identification: something that tells who a person is: *A driver's license or other identification often has the person's photo.*

problem: trouble.

sales: the department that sells a business's products. A person who sells things is *in sales.*

traveler's check: a check that you buy at a bank and that you can cash later in another city or country in many banks, restaurants, hotels, stores, etc. Only the person who buys the traveler's check can cash it.

MINI-CONVERSATION 1

A: Dad, Ron and I want to get married.
B: You're still too young.
A: Yes, but we love each other.
B: Love isn't everything. There are other things besides love.
A: Well, everybody thinks . . .
B: I don't want to hear what the others think. The answer is no. Forget it!

MINI-CONVERSATION 2

A: May I borrow some salt from you? I was on the phone all afternoon and forgot to go to the supermarket.
B: Certainly, Mrs. Sponge.
A: And can you lend me some sugar too?
B: Yes, I can lend you salt and sugar, but not another thing.

MINI-CONVERSATION 3

A: Operator, I want to make a collect call to Buenos Aires.
B: What number, please?
A: 234-5678
B: Who do you want to talk to?
A: Raul Martinez.
B: I'm afraid I can't hear you.
A: Raul Martinez. M-A-R-T-I-N-E-Z.
B: And your name, sir?
A: John Baker. And my number is 555-6543.
B: Hold the line, Mr. Baker. . . . I'm afraid the line is busy, sir. Can you try again in a few minutes? . . . Oh! One minute. It's ringing now.

CONVERSATION PRACTICE

About Conversation 1

1. Where does Mr. Sanchez work? 2. Which department? 3. What does Pablo want?
4. What did Mr. Sanchez use to do when he was Pablo's age? 5. Does Pablo have a license?
6. Is Mr. Sanchez going to lend him the car? 7. Why do you think Mr. Sanchez is angry?

About Conversation 2

1. What does Mr. Chen want to do? 2. What's wrong with his pen? 3. Does the clerk lend him hers? 4. How does Mr. Chen want the money? 5. Where's his passport? 6. Does he have any other identification? 7. Does he need identification to exchange Chinese money for American money?

Situation 1

You want to borrow some money from a friend.

Ask how he / she is.
    He / She answers.
Tell him / her you'd like to borrow some money.
    He / She asks how much you need.
Tell him / her how much.
    He / She wants to know why you need it.
Tell him / her why.
    He's / She's very sorry, but he / she can't lend you the money because . . . . .

Situation 2

You are making a telephone call.

You want to talk to Mr. Wilson.

    The operator says there are two Wilsons and asks what his first name is.

Tell her his first name and which department he works in.

    His number is busy. She asks you to hold the line.

Tell her you are busy and prefer to call again.

SUMMARY OF NEW WORDS

<u>VERBS: REGULAR</u>

to borrow / borrowed[1]   to carry / carried   to dial / dialed   to exchange / exchanged

<u>VERBS: IRREGULAR</u>   <u>AUXILIARY VERBS</u>

to begin / began   to hear / heard   to ring / rang   may

to hang up / hung up   to lend / lent[2]

<u>NOUNS</u>

age(s)	cloth(s)	driver's license(s)	operator(s)	problem(s)	sheep (sheep)
bill(s)	coin(s)	foreigner(s)	paper	receiver(s)	traveler's
call(s)	cow(s)	identification	pen(s)	sales	check(s)
change	department(s)	line(s)	pepper	salt	

<u>PRONOUNS</u>   <u>ADJECTIVES</u>   <u>ADVERBS</u>   <u>CONJUNCTIONS</u>

another / (the) others / each other   another / other   collect   again   besides

<u>PHRASES AND EXPRESSIONS</u>

to answer the phone   Forget it!   Hold the line.   May I . . . ?   on the phone

---

EXERCISES

Ask and answer. Note that *May* is formal; *Can* is informal. Use Cue Book Chart 1. Start with *(informal)* / *she* / **8** / *this cloth?* / *Yes, of course.* or: *(formal))* / *I* / **8** / *you a drink?* / *Thanks, but I'm waiting for my boyfriend.*

        STUDENT A: Can she buy this cloth?
        STUDENT B: Yes, of course.
    or: STUDENT A: May I buy you a drink?
        STUDENT B: Thanks, but I'm waiting for my boyfriend.

1. *(informal)* / I / **9** / another record? / Yes, sure.
2. *(informal)* / I / **10** / on the phone? / Yes, but not too loudly.
3. *(formal)* / we / **11** / next to you? / I think this seat is taken.
4. *(informal)* / the children / **12** / with each other? / Yes, sure. It's a big bed.
5. *(formal)* / I / **13**? / Only in the corridor.
6. *(formal)* / we / **14** / to the operator? / She's on another line now.
7. *(informal)* / I / **15** / here? / I'm sorry. I didn't hear you.

---

[1]NOTE: You **borrow** something **from** someone.
[2]NOTE: You **lend** something **to** someone.

8. *(formal)* / we / **16** / to the foreigners in your department? / There's only one.
9. *(informal)* / they / **17** / inside? / Certainly. That's no problem.
10. *(formal)* / I / **18** / home with you? / I'm going by taxi. Do you want to come?
11. *(informal)* / he / **19** / on your farm? / Well, we need someone who can look after the sheep.
12. *(formal)* / she / **20** / with this pen? / I'm afraid it doesn't work.

Grammar Summary

1. Auxiliary Verbs: Can / May

ABILITY

Can he weigh his package?

PERMISSION

May he ⎫
Can he ⎬ weigh his package?

2. Pronouns and Adjectives: Other / Another / Each Other / The Others

ADJECTIVES

She wants **another** sandwich.

He wants the **other** sandwiches.

PRONOUNS

I'd like **another,** please.

I like milk, but **the others** prefer tea.

They like **each other.**

DEVELOPING YOUR SKILLS

A. Use *another / other / each other / others.*

1. May I bring the ___ suitcase? I hate to carry this one because it's so heavy.
2. I want to make ___ call. Can you lend me a coin?
3. Why are the children arguing again? Because they just don't like ___.
4. Some people use a lot of salt when they cook; ___ prefer only a little.
5. Mr. and Mrs. MacDonald had sheep, cows, horses, and ___ animals on their farm.
6. The war began because the prime ministers didn't like ___.

7. If you don't have your driver's license, sir, why do you expect me to ask the ____ for theirs?
8. That wasn't the only trouble we had. There were many ____ problems besides that.
9. Operator! I'm afraid the line is bad. We can't hear ____.
10. ____ foreigner was robbed. They took his traveler's checks and all his bills. But they left some change so he could make a phone call.
11. Mary is looking for some ____ identification because she left her passport at the hotel.
12. Why don't you borrow some change from the ____? They always have a lot.
13. Excuse me a minute. The ____ phone is ringing.
14. I bought the wrong size, so I'd like to exchange this blouse for ____ one.

B. Complete the conversations.

1. A: . . . speak to Mr. Jackson?
   B: I'm afraid his line . . .
2. A: Can I . . . some money?
   B: Sorry, but I can't . . . you any.
3. A: Do you have a . . . ?
   B: No, I don't. I don't drive.
   A: Well, do you have any . . . ? We can't cash your check without it.
4. A: Why didn't you answer the phone?
   B: I'm sorry. I didn't . . . it.
5. A: . . . I . . . some . . . so I can type a letter?
   B: I don't have any. Why don't you ask Mr. Sanchez to . . . you some?
6. A: Did you talk to each . . . ?
   B: When I called him, the line . . .
   A: Maybe you dialed the wrong . . .

Reading

If you want to eat something, you need money. If you want to go somewhere, you need money. You just can't do anything without it anymore. But where did money begin?

Well, a long, long time ago people began to exchange things with each other. If someone had a cow and wanted some cloth, he exchanged the cow's milk for it. People could exchange
5 anything that someone else wanted and could use. So people in different places used different kinds of "money": sheep, fish, knives. The Japanese exchanged rice, the Chinese used tea, and in Ethiopia they used salt.

After many years people began to use gold, and then they made coins. But coins were heavy, and people didn't like to carry them, so they started to use paper money. They say the
10 Chinese first used paper money. Today checks are another kind of paper money—you sign your name and tell the bank to pay the other person.

Of course money can be a terrible problem. If you don't have any, you are really in trouble. But when you do have money, there are people who want to steal it—and sometimes kill you because they want or need it so much. So poor people are worried because they can't buy
15 things that they need and often can't borrow to pay their bills. And rich people are worried because maybe tomorrow they're going to be poor.

1. Why do people need money?   2. When people didn't have money what did they do?   3. What kinds of things did they exchange? What other kinds of things do you think they used?   4. Why didn't people like to have a lot of coins?   5. Who first used paper money? 6. Why is money sometimes a problem?   7. Are you worried when you don't have enough money? Do you ever have too much?   8. Why do people use traveler's checks?   9. Would you prefer to be rich or poor? Why?

Talk About Yourself

1. Do you think money is important? Why / Why not?   2. Do you often borrow things? What? Who do you borrow from?   3. Do you ever lend things? What? Who do you lend things to?   4. Do you have a driver's license? How old were you when you got it?   5. When do you need to use your identification? What kind of identification do you have?

Test Yourself

Finish the sentences. (1 point each)

1. That number is busy
2. Can I
3. Why don't you try
4. We love each other a lot
5. It's very noisy in here
6. I only have large bills, so I need
7. I don't want to hear
8. He plans
9. I don't love him anymore, and besides
10. Can you please sign here

a. some change.
b. what the others think.
c. so can you hold the line?
d. borrow your records?
e. to lend his stereo to Pepita.
f. but sometimes we argue.
g. and then may I see your identification?
h. to use some other kind of paper?
i. so I'm afraid I can't hear you.
j. I don't want to get married yet.

Total Score _____

What to say . . .

Can I borrow your car?

Of course not. Can't you see it isn't working?

LESSON 12

CONVERSATION 1

MRS. FRETTER: Oh, officer. We can't find our little Bobby anywhere.

OFFICER: Have you looked in the house, in the yard . . . ?

MRS. FRETTER: Yes, we have.

5   OFFICER: Have you asked your neighbors if they've seen him?

MRS. FRETTER: Yes. We've looked everywhere and spoken to all the neighbors. Oh, officer, I'm so worried!

10   OFFICER: What was he wearing?

MRS. FRETTER: He was wearing a red sweater.

OFFICER: What color pants?

MRS. FRETTER: No pants.

OFFICER: No pants? How old is Bobby?

15   MRS. FRETTER: He's only eighteen months.

OFFICER: Now don't worry, Mrs. Fretter. We're going to find your baby.

MRS. FRETTER: Our baby!? But Bobby isn't a baby. He's our dog.

CONVERSATION 2

MR. BEST: My boss is coming tonight. This party needs to be a big success. Do you understand?

JENNY & ALAN: Yes, Dad.

MR. BEST: Now, Alan, have you cleaned the yard and fixed the fence?

5   ALAN: Yes, Dad. I've already done it.

MR. BEST: Good! Jenny, have you washed all the dishes and the ashtrays?

JENNY: Yes, Dad. I've just finished.

10   MR. BEST: Fine! Darling, have you ironed my shirt?

MRS. BEST: Of course I've ironed it. And have you . . .

MR. BEST: . . . bought the wine! Oh, dear! I forgot.

New Words

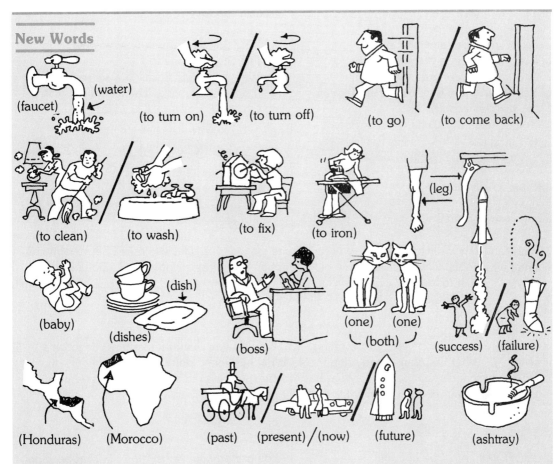

(faucet) (water)

(to turn on) (to turn off)

(to go) (to come back)

(to clean) (to wash)

(to fix) (to iron)

(leg)

(baby)

(dish)

(dishes)

(boss)

(one) (one)

(both)

(success) (failure)

(Honduras) (Morocco)

(past) (present)/(now)

(future)

(ashtray)

DEFINITIONS

already: in the past: *Are you going to clean your room or have you already cleaned it?*

to describe: to tell about; to tell what somebody or something is like.

just: now; a few minutes ago. *Do you want to talk to Tom? I just talked to him.*

to look: to turn your eyes so you can see; to go and see. (NOTE: **to look for:** to try to find.)

neighbor: person who lives or works near you.

to worry: to be worried.

MINI-CONVERSATION 1

A: Have you ever been to Honduras?
B: No, I haven't. Have you?
A: Yes, I have. I just came back from there.

MINI-CONVERSATION 2

A: Why don't you turn on the radio?
B: I just turned it on* a few minutes ago.
A: I guess it isn't working.
B: Or maybe someone else turned it off.

---

*NOTE: We can say **to turn on**/**off** the radio or **to turn** the radio **on**/**off**. But with a pronoun, we say **to turn** it **on**/**off**.

MINI-CONVERSATION 3

A: Have you ever eaten snails?
B: Yes, I ate some in Morocco.
A: And have you ever drunk tequila?
B: Yes, when I was in Mexico. And I loved the saké in Japan.
A: You've been everywhere. What do you do?
B: I'm a pilot.

CONVERSATION PRACTICE

About Conversation 1

1. Who can't Mrs. Fretter find? 2. Where has she looked? 3. Has she asked her neighbors? 4. What was Bobby wearing? 5. How old is Bobby? 6. Who is Bobby? 7. Do you think the officer is going to look for Bobby? Why?

About Conversation 2

1. Who is coming to the Bests' this evening? 2. Why do you think the party needs to be a success? 3. What has Alan already done? 4. What has Jenny done? 5. Has Mrs. Best ironed her husband's shirt yet? 6. What has Mr. Best forgotten to do? 7. Have you ever forgotten something for a party? What?

Situation 1

You can't find your little boy / girl.

Ask a neighbor if he's / she's seen him / her.
    He / She hasn't.
Ask someone you meet in the street.
    He / She asks what your child is like.
Describe him / her.
    The person asks what he / she was wearing.
Describe his / her clothes.
    He / She has just seen your child.
You ask where.
    He / She tells you and says what the child was doing.

MINI-CONVERSATION 4

A: Why don't you fix the faucet now?
B: I've already done it.
A: Well, I'm afraid it wasn't a success because it still isn't working. There's no hot water.
B: Oh, dear!

Situation 2

You are on your honeymoon in Europe. You are calling your parents. (Choose father or mother.)

Parent asks how and where you are.
    Tell him / her. Say you've just arrived.
Asks if you've had a good time.
    Tell him / her.
Asks which countries you've been to.
    Say which ones.
Says they haven't gotten any post cards yet.
    Tell him / her you sent some from . . .
Asks if you have bought many things.
    You've bought a lot of things. *(Tell what.)* Say you need some money and ask if they can send you some.
Says yes or no and tells you why.

SUMMARY OF NEW WORDS

OLD VERBS: IRREGULAR PARTICIPLES[1]

to be / was (were) / been[2]	to fly / flew / flown	to show / showed / shown
to become / became / become	to forget / forgot / forgotten	to sing / sang / sung
to begin / began / begun	to get / got / gotten	to speak / spoke / spoken
to break / broke / broken	to give / gave / given	to steal / stole / stolen
to choose / chose / chosen	to go / went / gone	to swim / swam / swum
to come / came / come	to know / knew / known	to take / took / taken
to do / did / done	to lie / lay / lain	to wake up / woke up / waked up
to drink / drank / drunk	to ring / rang / rung	to wear / wore / worn
to drive / drove / driven	to run / ran / run	to write / wrote / written
to eat / ate / eaten	to see / saw / seen	

NEW VERBS: REGULAR

to clean / cleaned / cleaned	to look / looked / looked	to wash / washed / washed
to describe / described / described	to turn on (off) / turned on (off) / turned on (off)	to worry / worried / worried
to fix / fixed / fixed		
to iron / ironed / ironed		

NEW VERBS: IRREGULAR   PRONOUNS   ADVERBS   PHRASES AND EXPRESSIONS

to come back / came back / come back   both   already   just   Oh, dear!

NOUNS

ashtray(s)	dish(es)	Honduras	neighbor(s)	saké	water
baby (babies)	failure(s)	leg(s)	past	success(es)	
boss(es)	faucet(s)	Morocco	present	tequila	

EXERCISES

A. Ask and answer. Use Cue Book Chart 6. Start with *you* (sing.) / **13** / *TV* (±).

> STUDENT A: Have you turned on the TV?
> STUDENT B: (+) Yes, I have. *or:* (−) No, I haven't.

1. the children / **14** / the faucet / (+)
2. you *(pl.)* / **15** / your coats yet / (−)
3. Mrs. Tanaka / **16** / already / (+)
4. you *(sing.)* ever / **17** / saké / (−)
5. the boys / **18** / to the swimming pool / (+)
6. Tommy / **19** / anything / (+)
7. Jenny / **20** / to her family / (−)
8. you *(sing.)* ever / **21** / (+)
9. your boss / **22** / you much work / (+)
10. the phone / **23** / today / (−)
11. you *(pl.)* / **24** / her the new ashtrays / (+)
12. Ms. Payne / **1** / any dishes / (−)
13. they / **2** / their new neighbors / (−)
14. he / **3** / the pen / (+)
15. we / **4** / our rooms well / (−)
16. they / **5** / my handkerchiefs / (−)

---

[1] See Grammar Summary.
[2] We call this third form the past participle. In the future we are going to show all three forms with new verbs: the infinitive, the simple past, and the past participle.

B. Ask and answer. Use Cue Book Chart 3. Start with *you* (sing.) / *to be to* / **13** (±)

STUDENT A: Have you been to the studio yet?
STUDENT B: (+) Yes, I've already been to the studio.
    or: (−) No, I haven't been to the studio yet.

1. the officer / to leave / **14** / (+)
2. Alan / to come back from / **16** / (−)
3. the bride and groom / to get to / **17** / (+)
4. the tourists / to see / **19** / (+)
5. their son / to write to / **20** / (−)
6. you *(sing.)* / to drive across / **21** / (−)
7. your boss / to go to / **22** / (+)
8. your neighbors / to eat out at / **23** / (−)
9. you *(pl.)* / to look in / **24** / (+)
10. the workers / to clean / **25** / (−)
11. the ladies / to choose / **26** / (+)
12. Mom / to give the check to / **27** / (+)
13. I / to take the dirty clothes to / **28** / (+)
14. the baby / to come back to / **29** / (−)

Grammar Summary

1. *Present Perfect Tense*

AFFIRMATIVE (+)

I've	(I + have)	
You**'ve**	(you + have)	
He**'s**	(he + has)	
She**'s**	(she + has)	already **been** there.
It**'s**	(it + has)	
We**'ve**	(we + have)	
You**'ve**	(you + have)	
They**'ve**	(they + have)	

NEGATIVE (−)

I, You } **haven't**
He, She, It } **hasn't** **been** there yet.
We, You, They } **haven't**

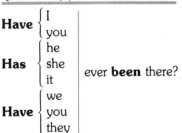

QUESTION (?)

Have { I / you

Has { he / she / it ever **been** there?

Have { we / you / they

SHORT ANSWER (+)

Yes, I / you } **have.**
he / she / it } **has.**
we / you / they } **have.**

SHORT ANSWER (−)

No, I / you } **haven't.**
he / she / it } **hasn't.**
we / you / they } **haven't.**

Have you been there **yet?** {
  Yes, **I have.**
  No, **I haven't.**
  No, **not yet.**

Have you **ever** been there? {
  Yes, **I have.**
  No, **I haven't** (**ever been** there).
  No, **I've never been** there.
  No, **never.**

NOTE: We use **yet** only in questions and in the negative. It usually comes at the end of the sentence. **Just** always comes between the auxiliary verb *have / has* and the main verb: *Have you just been there? Yes, I've just been there.* **Already** comes in either place: *Have you been there already? Yes, I've already been there.* **Ever** is used only in questions and in negatives: *Have you ever been there? Haven't you ever been there? Yes, I've been there / No, I've never been there / No, I haven't ever been there.* It comes after the auxiliary verb.

2. Present Perfect vs. Simple Past

When we use the simple past we usually suggest a definite time in the past: *I was in Paris six times last year.* The present perfect suggests an indefinite time in the past: *I've been in Paris six times.* We use the simple past only when something is not happening any more: *I was in Paris for two days (but I'm not there anymore).* When we use the present perfect it may or may not be still happening: *I've been in Paris (but I'm not there now)* or *I've been in Paris for two days (and I'm still there).*

3. Past Participles

There are four kinds of past participles. Here are some examples:

SAME AS SIMPLE PAST*	SAME AS INFINITIVE	END IN -EN, -N, -NE	HAVE I / A / U
to have / **had** / **had**	to **come** / came / **come**	to give / gave / **given**	to beg**i**n / beg**a**n / beg**u**n
to sit / **sat** / **sat**	to **hit** / hit / **hit**	to fly / flew / **flown**	to s**i**ng / s**a**ng / s**u**ng
& all regular verbs:	to **run** / ran / **run**	to go / went / **gone**	to sw**i**m / sw**a**m / sw**u**m
to ask / **asked** / **asked**			
to live / **lived** / **lived**			
to try / **tried** / **tried**			

DEVELOPING YOUR SKILLS

Use the right forms of the verbs to complete the conversations.

1. A: ＿＿ you ever ＿＿ something important? (to forget)
   B: Yes, I ＿＿. I ＿＿ to bring my books to class last week.
2. A: ＿＿ the doctor ＿＿ yet? (to come)
   B: Yes, he ＿＿. He ＿＿ a few minutes ago.
3. A: ＿＿ the show already ＿＿? (to begin)
   B: Yes, it ＿＿. It ＿＿ at 8:00.
4. A: ＿＿ the baby ＿＿ any water today? (to drink)
   B: No, he ＿＿.
   C: Yes, he ＿＿. He just ＿＿ some.
5. A: ＿＿ your aunt and uncle ＿＿ Professor Soares for a long time? (to know)
   B: Yes, they ＿＿. They ＿＿ him when they lived in Honduras.
6. A: Excuse me. ＿＿ you ever ＿＿ my boyfriend? (to meet)
   B: Yes, I just ＿＿ him. He's very good-looking.

---

*All verbs that you know that are not in the list of irregular past participles on page 85 follow this pattern.

7. A: Mother, ___ I ever ___? (to fly)
   B: Yes, you ___ to Japan with us when you were a baby.
8. A: ___ Lisa ___ any letters from Jack? (to get)
   B: No, I don't think she ___ ___ any.
   C: No, she ___. But she ___ a post card last week.
9. A: ___ Alan ___ his new suit? (to wear)
   B: I don't think he ___ ever ___ it.
   C: Yes, he ___. He ___ it to the Kanes' reception.
10. A: ___ the boys ever ___ in the Highland River? (to swim)
    B: It's so dirty, I hope they ___ ___ in it. Of course, we ___ in it many years ago.
11. A: ___ you ___ your room? (to clean)
    B: No, we ___. Mother ___ it yesterday.
12. A: ___ Jenny ___? (to come back)
    B: Yes, she ___ over an hour ago.
13. A: ___ you ___ to turn on the faucet? (to try)
    B: No, I ___. I ___ last night but it wasn't working.
14. A: I ___ ever ___ that show. ___ you? (to see)
    B: Yes, we ___ it last week.

Talk About Yourself

1. Have you ever had an accident? What happened? Describe the accident.   2. Have you ever been to a party that was a failure? What happened? Why didn't the guests have a good time? 3. Have you ever been robbed? Did they catch the thief? What did he / she steal?   4. Have you ever stolen anything? If you have, what did you steal?   5. Have you ever won or lost a lot of money? Tell about it.   6. Have you ever found anything? What did you find? Where did you find it?   7. Have you ever broken an arm / leg / etc.? What did you break? What happened?   8. Have you ever hit anybody? Who? Why? What happened then?   9. Have you ever eaten snails? / drunk tequila or saké? Where? Did you like them?

Test Yourself

Choose the right answers to the questions. (1 point each)

1. Is Mr. Tanaka in his office?	a. No, not many.
2. Have you ever been to Ceylon?	b. I haven't even gotten my driver's license yet.
3. What was it like?	c. For two weeks.
4. Is the radio still on?	d. Yes, she's already written them.
5. When do you plan to buy a car?	e. No, I haven't seen him yet.
6. Has Mary finished all the letters?	f. Last night.
7. How long have you had your new dishes?	g. No, I'm afraid I've lost them.
8. Have you found your glasses?	h. It was the best movie I've ever seen.
9. Have they broken a lot of things?	i. No, never.
10. When did James come back?	j. No, they turned it off before dinner.

Total Score _____

What to say . . .

Song   I'VE NEVER FOUND GOLD ANYWHERE

I've been to Jamaica
I've been to Japan
I've traveled all over the world.
I've gone on a ship
5 And I've flown in a plane
But I've never found diamonds or gold

I studied in Paris when I was nineteen
I looked for happiness there.
Then I went to London where I saw the queen
10 And rented a small room in Mayfair.
But I've never found gold anywhere
But I've never found gold anywhere.

I've been a waiter, a porter, a writer
I've been a singer, a driver, a fighter.

When I finished school I worked in a bank   15
Then I fought in a terrible war.
They thought I was lazy and gave me no rank
When I left I worked in a store
But I found it a terrible bore
But I found it a terrible bore.   20

I've been a waiter, a porter, a writer
I've been a singer, a driver, a fighter.

I've married and worried
About too many women
I've used all my money on them.   25
No bosses, no babies—I've lived for the ladies
I've chosen a life without care.
But I've never found love anywhere
But I've never found love anywhere.

Lesson 12   **eighty-nine/89**

LESSON 13

CONVERSATION 1

	HANS:	Have you been to the mountains yet?
	HELEN:	No, I haven't.
	HANS:	Are you busy this morning?
	HELEN:	Well, actually I . . .
5	HANS:	Would you like to go for a drive?
	HELEN:	I'd love to, but I have to do the housework, and then I have to wash my hair.
	HANS:	How about this afternoon? We can go for a walk or for a swim.
10	HELEN:	It's a great idea, but I have to write some terribly important letters.
	HANS:	Can't you do that some other time?
	HELEN:	I'm afraid I can't. I'm expecting my boss at 3 o'clock. He's going to help me.
15	HANS:	Well, I'd like to invite you for a meal tonight, then.
	HELEN:	That's really very kind of you, but unfortunately I have a date tonight. I'm going out with my boss. I just couldn't refuse. I'm awfully sorry, Hans. Maybe another time.

CONVERSATION 2

	TERESA:	Hello, Ingrid? This is Teresa.
	INGRID:	Hello, Teresa. We missed you last night.
	TERESA:	I'm terribly sorry, but Ken's sick. He felt awful when he got home and I had to call the doctor.
5	INGRID:	What's the matter with him? Nothing serious, I hope.
	TERESA:	No, fortunately not. The doctor thinks he's just working too hard. He's going to have to stay home for a few days. I'm sorry I didn't call last night, but I was so worried.
10	INGRID:	That's quite all right. I understand. I'm sure he's going to be fine soon. Thanks for calling. And give my regards to Ken.

New Words

(to do / wash (the) dishes)

(to do (the) housework)

(to do (your) homework)

(washing machine)

(to do (the) laundry)

(to get a haircut) (to get a shave)

(to shave)

(present)

(umbrella)

(mountain)

(plate)

(flower)

(invitation)

DEFINITIONS

actually: really.

awfully: terribly.

date: appointment to go out with someone. We usually use *appointment* for business: *I have an appointment with the personnel manager; I have a doctor's / dentist's appointment.** We usually use *date* when we are going to have a good time: *I had a date with Pete last night.*

to do (the) dishes: to wash / clean the dishes.

to do (your) homework: to do school work at home.

to do (the) housework: to clean inside the house.

to do the laundry: to wash dirty clothes.

electric: lamps, TVs, stereos, washing machines, and many clocks and radios are electric.

to go for a drive (swim, walk): to go driving (swimming, walking).

to have to: to need to.

to invite: to ask someone to go somewhere.

kind: nice.

to miss: to be sorry someone isn't there *(I missed you at the party)*; not to go somewhere *(I missed the party)*; not to be somewhere at the right time *(I missed the bus).*

perhaps: maybe.

---

*NOTE: We use the possessive only when we are talking about an appointment with a dentist or doctor: *a doctor's / dentist's* **appointment,** but an **appointment with** an *engineer / manager / travel agent, etc.*

> **quite:** certainly; very: *That's quite all right.*
> **to refuse:** to say no.
>   **soon:** in the near future.

MINI-CONVERSATION 1

A: Hello, darling. How do you feel today?
B: Fine, just fine.
A: Do you love me?
B: Of course I love you.
A: Even if I did something wrong?
B: What have you done?
A: I had an accident with your car.
B: Was it serious?
A: No. Fortunately I was driving very slowly.

MINI-CONVERSATION 2

A: Ron, I'd like to invite you for dinner on Saturday night. I hope you can come.
B: I'm afraid I have to refuse. I have another invitation for Saturday.
A: Perhaps some other time then?
B: Yes, of course.

MINI-CONVERSATION 3

A: What do you have to do this afternoon, darling?
B: I have to pay the electric bill and the water bill.
A: What! Haven't you paid them yet?
B: No, I'm awfully sorry, but I forgot.
A: Well, that's quite all right, if they aren't too late.

MINI-CONVERSATION 4

A: Where have you been?
B: I had to take Charles to the airport. He's gone to Indonesia.
A: Is he coming back soon?
B: Unfortunately he has to be there for a year.
A: Oh, what a shame! I'm going to miss him.

CONVERSATION PRACTICE

About Conversation 1

1. Has Helen been to the mountains yet?   2. Why can't she go for a drive?   3. What would Hans like to do in the afternoon?   4. What does Helen have to do then?   5. Who is she expecting? Why is he coming to her house?   6. What does Hans want to do tonight?   7. Why can't she go?   8. Do you think Helen really wants to go out with Hans? Why?

About Conversation 2

1. What's the matter with Ken?   2. What did Teresa have to do when he got home last night?
3. What does the doctor think is the matter?   4. What is Ken going to have to do?   5. Why didn't Teresa call Ingrid last night?   6. Who do you think is going to look after Ken?

Situation 1

A friend is inviting you to a party.

He / She says where and when and invites you.

     You have to refuse the invitation.

Situation 2

You missed a friend's dinner because you suddenly had to take a business trip with your boss. You are calling your friend.

Say the phone number while you dial.

You're expecting friends from . . .
He / She tells you to bring your friends too.
    You say he / she is very kind, but you
    have made other plans. *(Say what they
    are.)*
Your friend is going to miss you because . . .

Your friend answers the phone.
Say who you are. You just came back and are
sorry you missed the dinner. You hope he / she
got your note.
    He / She did. Thanks you for it and asks
    about your trip.
It was . . . You had to . . . Now you have to
rest for a few days.
    Your friend thanks you for calling.
Finish the call and hang up.

SUMMARY OF NEW WORDS

VERBS: REGULAR

to invite / invited / invited   to refuse / refused / refused   to shave / shaved / shaved
to miss / missed / missed

VERBS: IRREGULAR

to feel / felt / felt   to have to / had to / had to

ADJECTIVES

electric   great   kind   serious

NOUNS

date(s)	haircut(s)	invitation(s)	plate(s)	swim(s)	washing machine(s)
drive(s)	homework	laundry	present(s)	umbrella(s)	
flower(s)	housework	mountain(s)	shave(s)	walk(s)	

ADVERBS

actually   fortunately   perhaps   soon   unfortunately

ADVERBS OF DEGREE

awfully

PHRASES AND EXPRESSIONS

to do / wash (the) dishes   to do (the) laundry   That's (quite) all right.
to do (your) homework   to get a haircut / shave   That's very kind of (you).
to do (the) housework   to go for a drive / meal / swim / walk   Thanks for calling.

EXERCISES

A. Ask and answer. Use Cue Book Chart 7. Start with *you* (sing.) / *this afternoon* / **5** / *the rent.*

    STUDENT A: What do you have to do this afternoon?
    STUDENT B: I have to pay the rent.

1. the groom / downtown / **6**
2. you *(sing.)* / now / **7**
3. your father / before breakfast / **8**
4. your aunt / at the department store / **9**
5. Jenny / at the market / **10**
6. you *(pl.)* / for Ann's birthday / **11**

7. your girlfriend / this evening / **1**
8. her boyfriend / after dinner / **2**
9. you *(pl.)* / tonight / **3**
10. Mrs. Blake / every day / **4**
11. Hans / after lunch / **5** / the bill

B. Ask and answer. Use Cue Book Chart 1. Start with **7** / *my records* / *study for a test.*

> STUDENT A: Would you like to listen to my records?
> STUDENT B: I'd love to, but I have to study for a test.

1. **8** / these handkerchiefs / go to the bank first
2. **9** / chess / look after my little brother
3. **10** / with our band / talk to my parents first
4. **11** / for a few minutes / pick up some flowers
5. **12** / here tonight / write the wedding invitations
6. **14** / to the karate teacher / leave early tonight
7. **15** / under my umbrella / catch this bus
8. **16** / to the prime minister / don't have anything important to say to him
9. **17** / for the dessert / go back to the office

C. Say. Use Cue Book Chart 7. Start with *come* / **1.**

I'm sorry I couldn't come but I had to do the laundry.

1. call / **2**
2. see the show / **3**
3. meet your guests / **4**
4. go for a drive / **5** / the electric bill
5. go for a swim / **6**
6. kiss you / **7** / first
7. come back early / **8**
8. leave with you / **9**
9. wait / **10**
10. come this afternoon / **11** / for someone

Grammar Summary

1. Have to + Verb

AFFIRMATIVE (+)	NEGATIVE (−)
I **have to** work hard today.	I **don't have to** work hard today.
I **had to** work hard yesterday.	I **didn't have to** work hard yesterday.
I**'m going to have to** work hard tonight.	I**'m not going to have to** work hard tonight.
I **used to have to** work hard.	I **didn't use to have to** work hard.
I**'ve had to** work hard all my life.	I **haven't had to** work hard for a long time.

2. *Preposition:* For

For can tell *why:*

I go to restaurants **for** meals.	(= because I like to eat out)
Why do you work so much? **For** the money.	(= because I need the money)
Thank you **for** the invitation.	(= because you invited me)

For can tell *how long:*

> **(For)** How long did you stay?   **For** a minute (day, week, month, year).

For can tell *who you are giving something to:*

> This is a present **for** you, and I have some flowers **for** your mother too.

For is also part of some verbs:

What's he **looking for?** (For) His wallet.
Who's she **waiting for?** (For) Her neighbors.

DEVELOPING YOUR SKILLS

Use one of the following prepositions:

across   along   behind   for   in front of   into   over   without

1. Don't ever stand ___ someone who is cleaning a gun.
2. We lived in Honduras ___ ten years.
3. I'm not sure how old she is, but I think she's ___ fifty.
4. There was a student swimming ___ any clothes.
5. Mr. Wayne had an accident. He drove his car ___ the river.
6. Don't walk ___ the street when the traffic light is red.
7. We were driving ___ Main Street when the truck hit us.
8. The police officer didn't see the thief. He was standing ___ the curtain.

Talk About Yourself

1. What jobs did you have to do when you were a boy / girl?   2. What did you have to do in your first job?   3. Have you ever missed an important appointment? Why?   4. What do you have to do this week?   5. What are you going to have to do next week?   6. Where do you like to go when you have a date with someone? What do you like to do?   7. Do you ever go to the beach or the mountains? What for?

Test Yourself

Write. (2 points each)

1. You'd like to go for a . . . with a friend. What do you say?
2. Refuse an invitation.
3. Tell a friend why you couldn't go to his / her party.
4. You are talking to a friend. You look at your watch. It's very late and you need to go somewhere. What do you say?
5. A friend has been sick. What do you say when you see him / her?

Total Score _____

What to say . . .

LESSON 14

CONVERSATION

Ralph and Doris have just come back from a trip in the country.* They are talking to Kevin and comparing two towns that they visited: Boswell and Highland Springs.

KEVIN:　Which did you prefer, Boswell or Highland Springs?

RALPH:　Well, some things were better in one place, others were worse. But we liked them both. Have you been there?

KEVIN:　No, never.

5　DORIS:　I just loved Highland Springs. It isn't as busy as Boswell. It's cleaner, healthier, and the people are more relaxed.

RALPH:　And much friendlier.

KEVIN:　Is the cost of living higher in Boswell?

DORIS:　No, we found that things actually cost less there.

10　KEVIN:　That's strange! It's normally more expensive in bigger towns than in small places.

RALPH:　Yes, but unfortunately Highland Springs has become very popular with tourists, so everything is less expensive in Boswell.

KEVIN:　What's the weather like in that area?

DORIS:　It's much nicer in Highland Springs. You never know what to wear in Boswell.

15　RALPH:　When we first arrived we couldn't understand why everybody carried umbrellas.

DORIS:　But we soon found out.

RALPH:　Yes, when we left the hotel the next morning it was beautiful and sunny, and suddenly it became cloudy and began to rain.

KEVIN:　So the weather is very changeable.

20　DORIS:　Yes. From wet to wetter!

---

*Mexico, Japan, Morocco, etc., are all *countries*. But we also call an area that is not a city or town *the country* (always singular).

New Words

(the country)

(bee) (honey) (sweet)

(lemon) (sour)

$2+2=4$ $x^3-12x+8=0$

(easy) (difficult)

(healthy) (sick)

(relaxed)

(better) (good) (bad) (worse)

50 Q 7 Q

(cheap)

$E=mc^2$

(smart)

(comfortable)

(safe) (dangerous)

Danger

(tasty)

(friendly)

(cloudy) (sunny)

(wide) (narrow)

(wet) (dry)

DEFINITIONS

changeable: not always the same.

cheap: very inexpensive.

to cost: what you have to pay when you buy something is what it costs: *Expensive things cost a lot; inexpensive things don't cost much.*

cost of living: how much it costs to live.

fight: when people argue or hit each other.

to find out: to learn.

model: a new or old, small or large kind of product. *Kind of car:* Ford / *Model:* 1983 (*or:* small / four-door, etc.).

popular: when a lot of people like someone or something, he/she/it is popular.

relaxed: comfortable; not working or worrying.

strange: different or not what you expect.

tasty: delicious.

to visit: to go to see a person or place.

MINI-CONVERSATION 1

A: What kind of washing machine do you have?

B: Brand X.

A: Oh, it's the same as mine.

B: Yes, but yours is a newer model.

A: Well, they say you can't compare them because the older models are so much better than the new ones. You can wash much more in them.

MINI-CONVERSATION 2

A: I don't understand why you think Benny is going to win the fight.

B: Because he weighs more, he hits harder, and he's smarter than Clint.

A: Well, Clint is certainly a lot more popular than Benny.

B: I don't know why. He's not as good.

CONVERSATION PRACTICE

About the Conversation

1. Which town did Doris prefer? Why?   2. What did she and Ralph think of the people in Boswell?   3. Why is the cost of living less expensive there?   4. Is the weather better in Highland Springs?   5. Why did people carry umbrellas in Boswell?   6. Do you think Ralph and Doris would like to live in Boswell? Why or why not?

Situation

You and a friend are comparing the following things in your hometown(s) and other towns you've been to or know:

schools/universities	hotels	cost of living
libraries	restaurants	the weather
museums	theaters/movies	the people

SUMMARY OF NEW WORDS

VERBS: REGULAR

to compare / compared / compared
to visit / visited / visited

VERBS: IRREGULAR

to cost / cost / cost
to find out / found out / found out

NOUNS

bee(s)	fight(s)	lemon(s)
the country	honey	model(s)

ADVERBS

better	more
less	worse

PHRASES AND EXPRESSIONS

the cost of living
to know / understand why

ADJECTIVES

better	comfortable	easy	popular	sour	wet
changeable	dangerous	friendly	relaxed	strange	wide
cheap	difficult	healthy	safe	sweet	worse
cloudy	dry	narrow	smart	tasty	

COMPARATIVE EXPRESSIONS

as + *adj.* / *adv.* + as   less + *adj.* / *adv.* + than   more + *adj.* / *adv.* + than

EXERCISES

A. Ask and answer. Use Cue Book Chart 4 and the adjective form. Start with *detective* / **1.**

> STUDENT A: What was the other detective like?
> STUDENT B: He wasn't as careful as this one.

1. driver / **2**	4. drive / **5**	7. bees / **8**	10. story / **11**
2. flight / **3**	5. model / **6**	8. beds / **9**	11. babies / **12**
3. train / **4**	6. fight / **7**	9. bride / **10**	12. guests / **13**

B. Answer the questions. Use Cue Book Chart 8. Start with *that seat* / (+) *very* **1.**

> STUDENT A: Do you like that seat?
> STUDENT B: Yes, it's very comfortable.

1. this cheesecake / (−) too **2**
2. those oranges / (−) too **3**
3. your job / (+) very **4**
4. to take shorthand / (−) too **5**
5. the new bridge / (+) very **6**
6. Dr. Smith / (+) very **7**
7. to drive in the mountains / (−) too **8**
8. Mom's sauce / (+) very **9**
9. your boss / (−) not very **10**
10. the weather here / (+) very **11**
11. those necklaces / (−) not **12** enough
12. to play outside / (−) too **15**
13. this ring / (−) too **16**
14. guns / (−) not **17**
15. to carry an umbrella / (+) if it's **18**
16. Boswell / (+) very **19** there
17. that band / (+) very **20**
18. to eat with them / (+) always very **21**

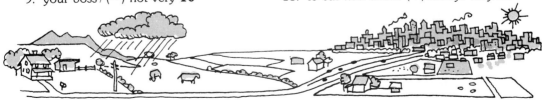

Grammar Summary

1. *Comparing People and Things with Adjectives*

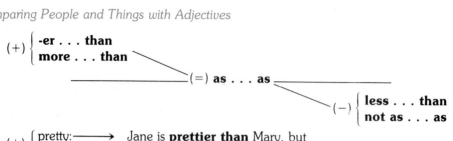

$(+)$ $\begin{cases} \text{pretty:} \longrightarrow \\ \text{popular:} \longrightarrow \end{cases}$ Jane is **prettier than** Mary, but
Mary is **more popular than** Jane.

$(-)$ $\begin{cases} \text{popular:} \longrightarrow \\ \\ \text{pretty:} \longrightarrow \end{cases}$ Jane is $\begin{cases} \textbf{less popular than} \\ \textbf{not as popular as} \end{cases}$ Mary, but

Mary is $\begin{cases} \textbf{less pretty than} \\ \textbf{not as pretty as} \end{cases}$ Jane.

$(=)$ pretty / popular: Cynthia is **as pretty and (as) popular as** Jane and Mary.

Adjectives of one or two syllables usually add -er. Use more with longer adjectives. BUT:
careful → more careful; careless → more careless; famous → more famous; relaxed →
more relaxed.
If the adjective ends in *e*: nic**e** → nic**er**; wid**e** → wid**er**.
If the adjective ends in *y*: prett**y** → prett**ier**; heav**y** → heav**ier**.
If a one-syllable adjective ends in one consonant: ho**t** → ho**tter**; we**t** → we**tter**.

NOTE: The adjectives *good* and *bad* have irregular forms: **good → better; bad → worse.**
We use them only in affirmative comparisons. In negative comparisons we use *not as
good / bad as* or *less good / bad than*.

2. *Comparing People and Things with Adverbs*

$(+)$ $\begin{cases} \text{fast:} \longrightarrow \\ \text{carefully:} \longrightarrow \end{cases}$ Jane runs **faster than** Mary, but
Mary runs **more carefully**.

$(-)$ $\begin{cases} \text{carefully:} \longrightarrow \\ \\ \text{fast:} \longrightarrow \end{cases}$ Jane $\begin{cases} \text{runs } \textbf{less carefully than} \\ \textbf{doesn't run as carefully as} \end{cases}$ Mary, but

Mary $\begin{cases} \text{runs } \textbf{less fast.} \\ \textbf{doesn't run as fast.} \end{cases}$

$(=)$ fast / carefully: Cynthia runs **as fast and (as) carefully as** Jane and Mary.

The adverbs *fast* and *hard* have affirmative forms that end in -er: **faster, harder.**
Most other adverbs use *more: more carefully, more quickly*, etc.
The adverbs *well* and *badly* have irregular forms: **well → better; badly → worse.**
We use them only in affirmative comparisons. In negative comparisons we use **not as
well / badly as** or **less well / badly than.**

NOTE: We also use *more* and *less* with verbs: I used **to eat more than** I do now. I **eat less
now than** I used to eat.

DEVELOPING YOUR SKILLS

A. Compare these two houses:

House A is cleaner than / not as dirty as House B.
House B is dirtier than / not as clean as House A.

1. modern	3. expensive	5. good	7. safe	9. pretty
2. large	4. warm	6. noisy	8. boring	10. wide

B. Ask and answer. Use Cue Book Chart 8 and the comparative form. Start with *you* (sing.). /
the test / 5.

STUDENT A: What did you think of the test?
STUDENT B: It was more difficult than I expected.

1. Mrs. Black / the new models / **6**
2. you *(pl.)* / the town / **7**
3. Mrs. Brown / the trip / **8**
4. Abdul and Alexandra / the shrimp / **9**
5. Ms. Collins / the manager / **10**
6. the tourists / the weather / **11**
7. your mother / the jewelry / **12**
8. you *(sing.)* / the cost of living / **13**
9. they / the fight / **14**
10. Mrs. Rich / the roads / **15**
11. Mr. Fisher / the river / **16**
12. the drivers / the roads / **17**
13. you *(pl.)* / the weather / **18**
14. Mr. Rodriguez / the turkey / **19**
15. Mrs. Best / the prime minister / **20**
16. you *(sing.)* / the actors / **21**
17. Ms. Tipsy / the couch / **1**
18. you *(pl.)* / the honey / **2**
19. the cooks / the lemons / **3**
20. the students / the questions / **4**

C. Ask and answer. Use Cue Book Chart 4. Start with *she sing / (+)***8**.

STUDENT A: How did she sing?
STUDENT B: She sang more loudly than she used to sing.

1. the band play / (−)**9**
2. he begin his work / (−)**10**
3. the car work / (+)**12**
4. the washing machine work / (−)**13**
5. they drive / (+)**1**
6. he carry the glasses / (−)**2**
7. you *(sing.)* run / (+)**3**
8. he sign his name / (−)**4**
9. they swim / (+)**5**
10. you *(pl.)* sleep / (+)**6**
11. your mother cook / (−)**6**
12. they sing / (+)**7**
13. his girlfriend dance / (−)**7**

Talk About Yourself

1. Do you prefer summer or winter? Why?   2. Do you prefer small towns or big towns? Why?   3. Do you prefer to travel by car or by bus? by train or by plane? Why?

Test Yourself

Make sentences. Use comparatives of the following words. (1 point each)

1. fast	3. slowly	5. dangerous	7. sunny	9. dry
2. smart	4. hot	6. narrow	8. well	10. bad

Total Score _____

What to say . . .

as busy as a bee

as quiet as a mouse

as happy as a clam

as sick as a dog

as healthy as a horse

as dry as a bone

as big as a house

as hungry as a bear

as pretty as a picture

LESSON 15

CONVERSATION 1

DR. BARNES:	Now, Mary, what's the matter?
MARY:	When I breathe I get this pain here in my chest.
DR. BARNES:	How long have you had it?
MARY:	Since last week.
5 DR. BARNES:	Does it hurt a lot?
MARY:	No, not really, but I feel something there.
DR. BARNES:	Take off your dress, Mary, and lie down. Let's have a look at you . . . Hmm! Have you met any good-looking boys lately?
10 MARY:	Why do you ask that?
MRS. MOORE:	What's wrong with her, doctor?
DR. BARNES:	I think it's her heart, Mrs. Moore.
MRS. MOORE:	It's nothing serious, is it?
DR. BARNES:	No, I don't think so. I think maybe your daughter's
15	in love.

CONVERSATION 2

DOCTOR:	How long have you had this cough?
PATIENT:	For two days.
DOCTOR:	And the fever?
PATIENT:	Since yesterday.
5 DOCTOR:	Does your body hurt?
PATIENT:	Oh, yes. My back, my legs . . . and I have an awful headache.
DOCTOR:	I'm afraid it's the flu.
PATIENT:	Do I have to take anything?*
10 DOCTOR:	Yes. Here's a prescription. Take two of these tablets every four hours. You must go to bed immediately and you mustn't get up before Monday.
PATIENT:	Monday! But the Lions are playing the Tigers on Sunday. I can't miss it.
15 DOCTOR:	And after you go to the game you're going to feel worse. I'm sorry, Mr. Clark. You're going to have to watch it on TV.

---

*Here, *to take* = to use medicine.

New Words

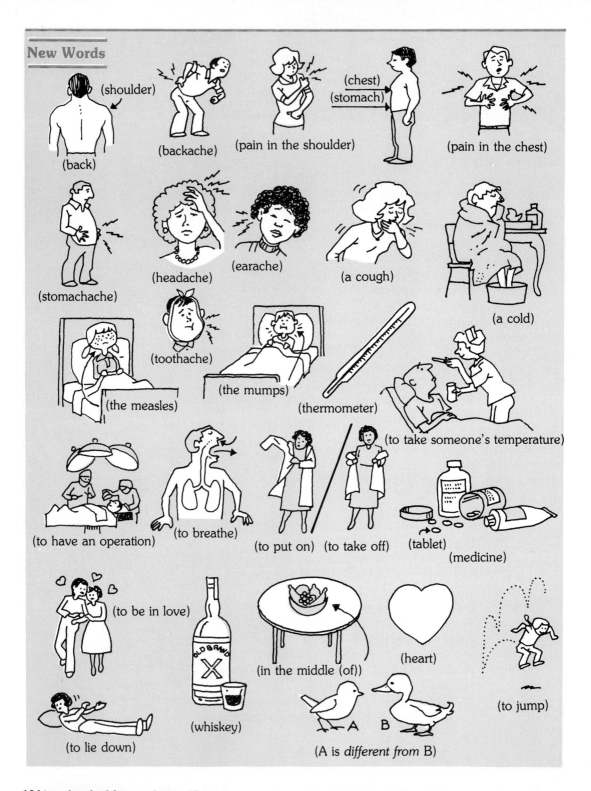

(shoulder)

(back)

(backache)

(pain in the shoulder)

(chest)
(stomach)

(pain in the chest)

(stomachache)

(headache)

(earache)

(a cough)

(a cold)

(the measles)

(toothache)

(the mumps)

(thermometer)

(to take someone's temperature)

(to have an operation)

(to breathe)

(to put on)   (to take off)

(tablet)

(medicine)

(to be in love)

(in the middle (of))

(heart)

(to jump)

(to lie down)

(whiskey)

(A is *different from* B)

DEFINITIONS

disease: sometimes when you are sick you have a *disease;* other times you just have an ache or a pain. Measles and mumps are diseases.

every + *time:* Every two hours = now, two hours later, then again two hours after that, etc. Every ten minutes = now, ten minutes later, then again ten minutes after that, etc.

to examine: to look carefully.

fever: high body temperature.

flu: a disease that is like a very bad cold but is more serious and dangerous. There is often a high fever, headache, stomachache, and aches in the arms, chest, back, and legs.

game: Soccer, tennis, and chess are games. There are also many different card games.

to get sick / well: to become sick / well.

glad: happy because of something.

to have a look at: to look at, to examine.

to hurt: to have an ache or pain somewhere.

lately: a short time ago.

must: to have to, to need to.

patient: sick person; any person—sick or well—who a doctor examines.

prescription: medicine that the doctor says you must take.

since: from a time in the past to now (used with the simple past and the present perfect tenses): *I have been sick since Saturday.* = *I began to be sick on Saturday and I'm still sick.*

uncomfortable: not comfortable.

what's wrong (with): what's the matter (with).

MINI-CONVERSATION 1

A: Hi, Fred. I haven't seen you for a long time. Where have you been?
B: I've been in the hospital. I had an operation.
A: How do you feel?
B: Well, I'm still breathing.

MINI-CONVERSATION 2

A: How's your stomach this morning?
B: Much better, thanks.
A: Oh, I'm glad. But you must stay in bed for another day or two, and you mustn't eat too much.
B: But, doctor, I haven't eaten anything since the day before yesterday.

MINI-CONVERSATION 3

A: Have you had that terrible disease that everyone's getting?
B: Yes, unfortunately, I have. I got terribly sick.
A: How long does the treatment last?
B: It lasts for about a month and it's worse than the disease.
A: But you got well. That's the important thing. One of my friends died.

CONVERSATION PRACTICE

About Conversation 1

1. How long has Mary had the pain? Where is it? 2. Does it hurt a lot? 3. What must Mary do before the doctor examines her? 4. What's the matter with her? 5. Do you think the doctor has a prescription for Mary? What prescription?

About Conversation 2

1. How long has Mr. Clark had the cough? 2. How long has he had the fever? 3. What hurts? 4. What's wrong with him? 5. What must he do? 6. What mustn't he do?
7. What's happening on Sunday? 8. Where do you think Mr. Clark is going to be on Sunday?

Situation 1

You are at the doctor's.

He / She asks what's wrong.
    Tell him / her.
Doctor asks how long you've had it.
    Tell him / her.
Asks if it hurts a lot and if you've ever had it before.
    Say yes or no. Ask what's wrong with you.
Doctor tells you, gives you a prescription, and tells you what you must / mustn't do.

Situation 2

You are talking to a friend who is overweight. Tell him / her what he / she must / mustn't do.

How long have you had this?

SUMMARY OF NEW WORDS

VERBS: REGULAR

to breathe / breathed / breathed
to examine / examined / examined

to jump / jumped / jumped
to last / lasted / lasted

ADJECTIVES

glad
uncomfortable

VERBS: IRREGULAR

to hurt / hurt / hurt
to lie down / lay down / lain down
to take off / took off / taken off

ADVERBS

lately
in the middle

PREPOSITIONS

because of
in the middle of
since

CONJUNCTIONS

after
before
since

NOUNS

ache(s)	cough(s)	headache(s)	pain(s)	tablet(s)
back(s)	disease(s)	heart(s)	patient(s)	temperature(s)
backache(s)	earache(s)	the measles	prescription(s)	thermometer(s)
body (bodies)	fever	medicine	shoulder(s)	toothache(s)
chest(s)	the flu	the mumps	stomach(s)	treatment(s)
cold(s)	game(s)	operation(s)	stomachache(s)	whiskey

AUXILIARY VERBS	PHRASES AND EXPRESSIONS	
must(n't)	to be in love	to have an operation
	different from	to take someone's temperature
	to get sick / well / a disease	What's wrong with . . . ?
	to have a look at	

EXERCISES

A. Use the right word or expression to answer.

1. A: When did you have to have the operation?
   B: *(In the middle of May. / Since May.)*
2. A: I have a backache, my legs hurt, and I have an awful cough.
   B: *(Maybe you have the flu. / Perhaps you have a pain.)*
3. A: What do you do when you have a headache?
   B: *(I usually get a disease. / I usually take two of these tablets and lie down.)*
4. A: Have you done anything interesting lately?
   B: *(No, not since I saw you last week. / No, not before I saw you last week.)*
5. A: I don't feel very good.
   B: *(Don't breathe so much. / Don't jump up and down anymore.)*
6. A: Dr. Barnes is terribly overweight, isn't he?
   B: *(Yes, his stomach is enormous. / Yes, his shoulders are enormous.)*
7. A: What's wrong?
   B: *(I have a fever. / I have a thermometer.)*
8. A: I feel much better today.
   B: *(I'm so glad. / I'm so uncomfortable.)*
9. A: Is a cold different from the flu?
   B: *(Oh, yes. It's much less serious. / Oh, yes. It's much more dangerous.)*
10. A: I had to take off all my clothes so the doctor could have a look at me.
    B: *(Did he examine you carefully? / Did you have many patients?)*
11. A: Do you ever take any medicine?
    B: *(Only when the doctor gives me the measles. / Only when the doctor gives me a prescription.)*
12. A: I'm glad the treatment was a success.
    B: *(Yes, I haven't had a stomachache since last Monday. / Yes, those games really bore me.)*
13. A: When the pain comes, does it last long?
    B: *(No, not since I got sick. / No, only a minute or two.)*

B. Ask and answer. Use Cue Book Chart 9. Start with *Pablo / 14 / Friday.*

> STUDENT A: What's wrong with Pablo?
> STUDENT B: He has the mumps.
> STUDENT A: How long has he had them?
> STUDENT B: He's had them since Friday.

1. Ali / **1** / you started playing your guitar
2. Pepita / **2** / she got up

3. you *(sing.)* / **3** / I came back from school
4. Ms. Smith / **4** / she ate that duck
5. Mr. Rodriguez / **5** / he woke up
6. Mrs. Ferrari / **6** / the accident
7. Pierre / **7** / he met Alexandra
8. Mr. Wilson / **8** / he played those games with the children
9. Nick / **9** / he started to smoke
10. Ms. Garcia / **10** / the operation
11. you *(sing.)* / **11** / I went out in that terrible rain
12. Sophia and Abdul / **12** / last week
13. your daughter / **13** / she played with your little boy

C. Ask and answer. Use Cue Book Chart 7. Start with (±) / *Fernando* / **6.**

> STUDENT A: What must *(or: mustn't)* Fernando do?
> STUDENT B: He must *(or: mustn't)* get a haircut.

1. (+) / Mr. Robinson / **7**
2. (−) / Mr. Chen / **8**
3. (+) / you *(pl.)* / **9**
4. (−) / the guests / **10**
5. (−) / you *(sing.)* / **11**
6. (−) / Mr. Smith / **1**
7. (−) / the waiter / **2**
8. (+) / the children / **3**
9. (+) / Alexandra / **4**
10. (−) / Mr. and Mrs. Ali / **5** / that bill
11. (−) / Maria / **6**

Grammar Summary

1. Auxiliary Verb: Must / Mustn't

I You } hurt.	I You		I You	
He She } hurts. It	He She } **must** have treatment. It		He She } **mustn't** wait. It	*(must + not)*
We You } hurt. They	We You They		We You They	

NOTE: We don't use *to* between *must* and the verb: *I **have to take** / **must take** these tablets.* Note that *must = to have to,* but *mustn't ≠ doesn't / don't have to.* **Mustn't** = can't even if you want to; **doesn't / don't have to** = can if you want to, but don't need to.

2. Prepositions: For / Since

For tells how long. *Since* tells when something (that has not finished yet) began:

> Mr. Brown bought the car in 1982. He still has the car.

PAST	PRESENT	FUTURE
	He's had the car **for . . . years.**	
1982 ├──────────────────────────── now ──→ ???		
	He's had the car **since 1982.**	

3. Prepositions and Conjunctions: Before / After / Since

We use *before, after,* and *since* as prepositions:

They took my temperature **before the operation.**
I always lie down **after a swim.**
The cost of living has been high **since June.**

We also use them as conjunctions before a subject and verb:

They took my temperature **before I had the operation.**
I always lie down **after I go swimming.**
The cost of living has been high **since Mr. Bull became president in June.**

4. The Word Of

We use *of* in many expressions before nouns and pronouns. It can change an adverb, a conjunction, etc., to a preposition:

The thermometer is **on top.** It's **on top of** the books.
The thermometer is **in the middle.** It's **in the middle of** the table.
There are **a lot,** aren't there? Of what? **A lot of** books.
He's happy **because** it's so sunny. **Because of** that he can play tennis.
I want that one **instead. Instead of** what? **Instead of** the other one.

We also use *of* after numbers to describe a small group that is in a larger group:

I have many friends. Only **three of them** speak English.
There are a lot of tablets in the bottle. I take **two of those** before I eat.

DEVELOPING YOUR SKILLS

A. Use *for* or *since* in the following sentences.

1. Mr. and Mrs. Duke have been married _____ ten years.
2. Rex King has refused to come back _____ he had that awful failure last year.
3. Ms. Short has worn glasses _____ 1978.
4. Nick and Alexandra have been in love _____ years.
5. I haven't seen my sister _____ she became a flight attendant.
6. Mary's had that ring _____ a long time.
7. The fight only lasted _____ twenty minutes.
8. Dr. Barnes hasn't bought any flowers _____ his wife died.
9. You haven't been there _____ the war started, have you?
10. My son hasn't done his homework _____ weeks.
11. Has Mrs. Van had this job _____ she left the university?
12. Ann hasn't visited us _____ many years.

B. Say. Use Cue Book Chart 1 and *since* or *for*. Start with *I / **1** / my boss / more than a month.*

I haven't argued with my boss for more than a month.

1. I / **2** / I got married
2. Mr. Webb / **3** / whiskey / 1970
3. Ms. Tanaka / **4** / she had her operation
4. the patients / **5** / meat / a month
5. Mr. Bass / **6** / over a year
6. we / **7** / any good music / someone stole our records
7. I / **8** / any tablets / two days
8. Mrs. Grump / **9** / tennis / she was a young girl
9. Mr. Byrd / **10** / in the bath / a long time
10. the children / **11** / on the floor / we bought the armchairs
11. we / **12** / in a comfortable bed / more than a week
12. Pete / **13** / he left the hospital
13. Mrs. Love / **14** / about her heart / months

C. Tell the people they must or mustn't do these things.

1. Tell Student A to come to class earlier.
2. Tell Student B not to smoke.
3. Tell Students A and B not to argue.
4. Tell Student A that Student B has to work harder.
5. Tell your teacher to help you more.
6. Tell Student A that Students B and C have to do their homework.
7. Tell the others you have to study more often.
8. Tell the others you and Student A have to answer questions more often.
9. Tell Students A and B not to forget to come to class next week.
10. Tell the others you have to do the laundry after class.
11. Tell the others what you really have to do tonight.

Reading

I've been in bed because I've had the flu. Flu is another name for influenza. It's a very uncomfortable disease. The patient usually has a high fever, bad headaches, and aches in the shoulders, back, arms, and legs. Sometimes there are also stomachaches and other stomach problems. You have to stay in bed. But that's no problem because you really don't want to do
5 anything else. The disease is not usually too dangerous, but older people and babies must be careful. Not many people have died from the flu lately, but in 1918 there was a terrible epidemic* and millions of people died.

Colds are different from the flu. The temperature is lower (often there is no fever), and you don't have as many aches and pains. Sometimes if you are already weak because of a bad cold,
10 you can also get influenza. It usually lasts from three to ten days.

---

*Epidemic = a disease that many people get at the same time.

People use many different kinds of treatments for colds and the flu. They sleep a lot, take hot baths, drink tea with lemon, hot milk, and even whiskey. When my wife had a cold in the middle of winter, she jumped into a swimming pool and the next day she said she felt better. My brother drank a bottle of whiskey, but that treatment was a failure. The next day he had an awful headache—and he still had his cold. There is really no special treatment for colds. A friend of mine, who is a doctor, always says: "A cold lasts for a week with treatment and seven days without it."

About the Reading

1. Where has the writer been? 2. What was wrong with him? 3. Describe the flu. 4. Do many people die from flu nowadays? 5. How long does the flu usually last? 6. What kinds of treatments do people use? 7. Have you ever used any special treatment? Was it a success? 8. How did the writer's wife feel after she jumped into the swimming pool? 9. How did the writer's brother feel after his treatment? 10. Does the writer's friend who is a doctor think that treatment helps a cold last a shorter time?

Talk About Yourself

1. Have you ever had the flu / measles / mumps / an operation? 2. How long has it been since you had the flu? 3. What must you do when you have the flu? What mustn't you do? 4. How long has it been since you went to a doctor? Did he / she examine you? Were you healthy? 5. Do you have a car / bike / motorbike / camera / stereo? How long have you had it? 6. Are you married? When did you get married? How long have you been married? 7. How long have you lived in your house / apartment / this town? 8. How long have you studied English?

Test Yourself

Ask questions to the following answers. (2 points each)

1. . . .
   Buster became a robber ten years ago.
2. . . .
   He's been a robber for ten years.
3. . . .
   No, he's never been in jail.

4. . . .
   He got married to Flo a few years ago.
5. . . .
   They've been married since 1981.

Total Score _____

What to say . . .

LESSON 16

CONVERSATION 1

INTERVIEWER: Now, Mrs. Abdala, what brand of toothpaste do you use in your home?

MRS. ABDALA: Brand X. I've used it for years. I used it before I got married, and now my whole family uses it.

5 INTERVIEWER: Have you tried other brands?

MRS. ABDALA: Yes, but they aren't as good. Brand X is the best toothpaste I've ever used.

INTERVIEWER: I'm glad to hear that. I . . .

MRS. ABDALA: Yes, it has a better taste, it makes your teeth
10 whiter, and it gives you the cleanest breath you've ever had.

INTERVIEWER: And what do you think of the price?

MRS. ABDALA: It's certainly the least expensive brand on the market.

15 INTERVIEWER: Thank you, Mrs. Abdala.

CONVERSATION 2

BILL: Nice, isn't she?

GARY: Beautiful. I just love her style.

BILL: Yes, it was love at first sight.

GARY: Are you happy with her?

5 BILL: She's the very best. I've been everywhere with her.

GARY: And has she ever given you trouble?

BILL: No, not really.

GARY: Is she comfortable?

BILL: Oh, much more comfortable than the others.

10 GARY: And expensive?

BILL: Oh, no! She's the most economical car on the road.*

———
*NOTE: We sometimes use *she* for cars, boats, planes, etc.

New Words

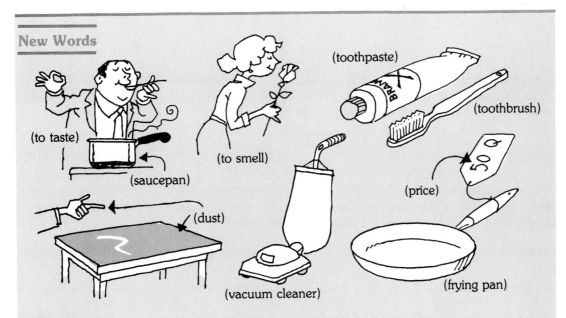

(to taste) (to smell) (toothpaste) (toothbrush) (saucepan) (price) (dust) (vacuum cleaner) (frying pan)

DEFINITIONS

brand: kind of product: *Ford is a brand of car; General Electric is a brand of refrigerator.*

breath: the air you breathe in and out.

economical: inexpensive to use.

least / most: Brand A costs 5Q; Brand B costs 7Q; Brand C costs 10Q. Brand A is the least expensive; Brand C is the most expensive.

love at first sight: when you love someone or something immediately the first time you see him / her / it.

on the market: when you can buy something in stores, markets, etc.

out: not in.

price: how much something costs.

smell: how something smells: *When you smell something that smells good, it has a nice smell.*

taste: how something tastes: *When you taste something that tastes delicious, it has a good taste.*

whole: all. My whole family = all my family; the whole sandwich = all of the sandwich.

MINI-CONVERSATION 1

A: What do I smell?

B: I'm cooking.

A: It sure smells good. What is it?

B: Shrimp. And if you like the smell, you'll love the taste. Would you like some?

A: Yes, please. Man! That tastes delicious. That's the best shrimp I've ever tasted.

MINI-CONVERSATION 2

A: *(sneezing)* Atchoo! . . . Atchoo!

B: Bless you.

A: Thank you.

B: It's the worst winter we've had for a long time. I have a cold too, and I've had it for more than a month now.

A: But I don't have a cold. It's the dust in the air.

B: Why don't you buy a vacuum cleaner then?

CONVERSATION PRACTICE

About Conversation 1

1. What brand of toothpaste does Mrs. Abdala use?   2. Has she used it for a long time?
3. Has she tried any other brands?   4. What does she think of them?   5. Is Brand X very expensive?   6. What brand of toothpaste do you use? Why? Does it taste good? Does it clean your teeth well? Does it clean your breath?

About Conversation 2

1. What are Gary and Bill talking about?   2. Is Bill happy with his car?   3. What does he say about it?   4. Has he ever had any trouble with it?   5. Do you have a car? How is it? Do you ever have any trouble with it? Is it comfortable? economical?

Situation 1

Talk with a friend. Tell him / her what you think of a famous product (a car or a camera, a brand of toothpaste or soap, etc.). Compare it to another brand. If your friend thinks differently, argue with him / her.

Situation 2

A salesman arrives at your door. He wants to show you a new model vacuum cleaner.
　　　You already have one and you're very happy with it. You've had it since . . .
He says his is the best. It is . . . , the least . . . , and the most . . .
　　　You don't want to buy it.
He tries to sell you an electric frying pan.
　　　You don't want one. Tell him why.
He still tells you about it.
　　　You are very sorry, but you have to go. Say why, then say good-by.

SUMMARY OF NEW WORDS

VERBS: REGULAR

to smell / smelled / smelled   to sneeze / sneezed / sneezed   to taste / tasted / tasted

NOUNS

air	dust	price(s)	taste	vacuum cleaner(s)
brand(s)	frying pan(s)	saucepan(s)	toothbrush(es)	
breath(s)	pan(s)	smell(s)	toothpaste	

ADJECTIVES   ADVERBS

the best	economical	whole	the worst	(the) least	the most	out

PHRASES AND EXPRESSIONS

atchoo!   Bless you!   love at first sight   on the market

EXERCISES

Use the right word or expression to finish the sentences.

1. After someone sneezes, you say *("Atchoo!"/"Bless you.")*
2. You have to do the housework more often in the summer when there's a lot of *(air/dust)*.
3. I made fried fish in my new *(frying pan/saucepan)*.
4. Most flowers *(smell/taste)* nice.
5. Toothpaste cleans your teeth and your *(breath/taste)*.
6. I don't buy anything if the *(brand/price)* is too high.
7. This is a great product, but unfortunately it's very *(economical/expensive)* too.
8. You clean your mouth with a *(toothbrush/vacuum cleaner)*.
9. I love this couch. It's *(the least/the most)* comfortable one I've ever sat on.
10. You're going to enjoy this washing machine. It's *(the best/the worst)* one on the market.

Grammar Summary

Superlative Adjectives and Adverbs

pretty: Jane is **pretty.** Mary is even **prettier,** but she's **less pretty than** Cynthia. Cynthia is **the prettiest** girl in the class.

popular: Jane is **popular.** Mary is even **more popular,** but she's **less popular than** Cynthia. Cynthia is **the most popular** person in the school. Jane is **the least pretty** and **the least popular** (of the three).

fast: Jane runs **fast.** Mary runs **faster.** But Cynthia runs **the fastest.**

carefully: Jane runs **carefully.** Mary runs **more carefully.** But Cynthia runs **the most carefully.** Jane runs **the least fast** and **the least carefully.**

Adjectives and adverbs of one or two syllables usually add *-est.* Use *most* with longer adjectives and adverbs. BUT: the most careless, the most careful, the most famous, the most relaxed.

If the adjective ends in e: nic**e** → nic**er** → the nic**est;** wid**e** → wid**er** → the wid**est.**

If the adjective ends in y: pretty → pretti**er** → the pretti**est;** heavy → heav**ier** → the heav**iest.**

If a one-syllable adjective ends in one consonant: gla**d** → gla**dder** → gla**ddest;** wet → wetter → we**ttest.**

NOTE: The adjectives *good* and *bad* and the adverbs *well* and *badly* have irregular forms:
   good/well → better → the best; bad/badly → worse → the worst.

DEVELOPING YOUR SKILLS

A. Use Cue Book Chart 8. Start with **17**/road/I/to drive on.

It's the safest road I've ever driven on.

1. **18**/day/I/to see
2. **19**/summer/we/to have
3. **20**/movie/he/to make
4. **21**/person/I/to know
5. **1**/bed/Mr. Flap/to sleep in
6. **2**/orange/Ms. Sanchez/to eat

7. **3** / lemon / I / to taste
8. **4** / job / Omar / to do
9. **5** / thing / Ann / to learn
10. **6** / plane / Yoko / to fly in
11. **7** / dog / we / to see
12. **8** / corner / Mr. Gunn / to work at
13. **9** / toothpaste / I / to try
14. **10** / saleswoman / we / to meet
15. **11** / day / we / to have
16. **12** / model / they / to make
17. **13** / price / we / to have
18. **14** / frying pan / they / to sell

B. Use the right form of the words.

1. The Dove's Inn is *(less)* comfortable hotel in our city.
2. I'm afraid Mr. Barber is *(smart)* than I expected.
3. My husband drives *(dangerous)* than I do.
4. These are certainly *(pretty)* flowers in the store.
5. Johnny is a much *(bad)* player than his brother.
6. Do you always speak so *(quick)*?
7. Our receptionist doesn't work as *(hard)* as she used to.
8. Our neighbor's daughter Mary was *(sad)* child I've ever seen.
9. Sugar isn't as *(sweet)* as honey.
10. Our plane arrived *(early)* than yours.
11. This is *(good)* frying pan I've ever used.
12. Mr. Hope is *(important)* man in our country.

Talk About Yourself

1. Talk about the best / worst meal you've ever had.   2. Talk about the best / worst movie you've ever seen.   3. Can you remember the worst problem you've ever had? What happened?   4. What was the best thing that ever happened in your life?   5. Which do you think is the best car on the market? Why?   6. Who eats the most in your family? Who works the least? Who sleeps the most?

Test Yourself

Fill in the following table. (½ point each)

ADJECTIVE / ADVERB	COMPARATIVE	SUPERLATIVE
1. _____	_____	the most quickly
2. _____	more uncomfortable	_____
3. famous	_____	_____
4. hard	_____	_____
5. _____	uglier	_____
6. _____	_____	the worst
7. good	_____	_____
8. _____	faster	_____
9. badly	_____	_____
10. _____	_____	the least beautiful

Total Score_____

What to say . . .

> It's the heaviest darn thing I've ever carried.

Song   GUESS WHAT IT IS

<pre>
      D   A7
It's colder and creamier
    Bm   F♯
It's better and tastier
    D   A7
Than all the things that I've had
      D   A7
It's heavier than water
      Bm   F♯
But lighter than butter
      D   A7
And much more delicious than bread
                  B
So guess what it is.
</pre>
(5 marks line 5)

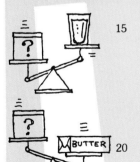

<pre>
          D
15 Blood is thicker than wine
          G
    Lemon is sourer than lime
          A7
    Honey's the sweetest thing

    You can find
              G   D
    And secrets are best in your mind
          D
20 Diamonds are brighter than gold
          G
    Troubles are heavier than lead
              A7
    And the years go by

    Much faster than lightning
              G   D
    Some people are better when dead . . .
              A7
25 When they're dead.
</pre>

<pre>
        D   A7
It's slower than horses
    Bm   F♯
It's cheaper than buses
    D   A7
But so much louder than trains
    D   A7
It's faster with one on
      Bm   F♯
It's easier to stay on
    D   A7
Than on a bike when it rains
              B
So guess what it is.
</pre>
(10 marks line 10)

LESSON 17

CONVERSATION

MANAGER: Can I help you, sir?

GUEST: Yes, please. I want another room.

MANAGER: I'm afraid we don't have another room free right now. Is anything wrong?

5   GUEST: Yes. The shower isn't working.

MANAGER: Why don't you take a bath instead, sir?

GUEST: That's another problem. There's no hot water.

MANAGER: Oh, dear! I *am* sorry, sir . . . But don't worry. We'll do our best. Charlie! Take some hot water up to 201.

10   GUEST: And I'll need some soap. There isn't any there.

MANAGER: I'll send some up immediately. Charlie! Some soap too! I'm terribly sorry about that, sir. It won't happen again.

GUEST: Well, I hope not. And can someone change the towels? They're dirty.

15   MANAGER: Charlie! Don't forget some clean towels. There are none in 201 . . . I apologize, sir.

GUEST: Look, I must complain to the manager about the service in this place.

MANAGER: I'm the manager.

20   GUEST: I see. This is a four-star hotel, isn't it?

MANAGER: Oh, no, sir! We don't have any stars at all.

GUEST: Then why do you have those four stars outside?

MANAGER: That's just our name, sir: The Southern Cross.*

———

*The Southern Cross:

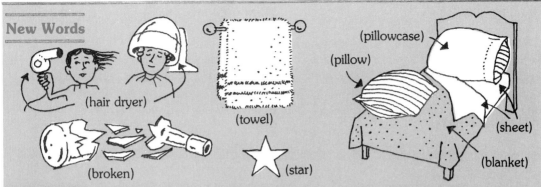

New Words

(hair dryer)

(towel)

(pillowcase)

(pillow)

(sheet)

(blanket)

(broken)

(star)

DEFINITIONS

to apologize: to say you're sorry.

  as soon as possible: as soon as you can.

to change: to make something different *(He changed the picture)*; to become different *(John has really changed, hasn't he?)*; to take one thing and put another one in its place *(I want to change my clothes)*.

to complain: to say that something is bad, wrong, or not working.

to do your best: to try to do everything you can.

  free: something that no one is using is free *(Is that table free?)*; not busy *(Go right in. The doctor is free now)*.

  in a hurry: when you want or need to do something immediately.

  in a minute: very soon.

  no good: bad; not good.

  none: not any.

  not . . . at all: This expression makes a negative verb, an adjective, or an adverb stronger: *I'm not happy at all. / I'm not at all happy. This hair dryer doesn't work (well) at all. / This hair dryer doesn't work at all (well).*

  ready: when you have finished something; when you can do something right away.

    NOTE: **to have something ready** = to be ready to give something to someone.

  receipt: paper that you get when you buy something or pay a bill. It says you have paid.

  right now: immediately.

  service: how people help you in a hotel, store, business, etc.; how well a business does its job.

MINI-CONVERSATION 1

A: Can I help you, ma'am?

B: Yes, I want to complain about these towels. I bought them here three weeks ago, and just look at them! They're no good at all.

A: Do you have your receipt?

B: Yes. Here it is.

A: I'll talk to the manager. I'm sure he'll exchange them for you.

MINI-CONVERSATION 2

A: Darling, will you do the dishes? I have to go now.

B: Of course, I will. I hate to see you go out. Will you be late?

A: I'm afraid so. I don't think I'll be home before midnight.

B: All right. Good-by, darling. *(She leaves; he dials the phone.)* Mike, this is John. I'm ready. You and the others can come now.

MINI-CONVERSATION 3

A: My shoe is broken. Can you fix it for me?
B: Sure, miss. I'll do it as soon as possible.
A: But I need it now. I'm in a terrible hurry.
B: All right. I'll do it in just a minute.

MINI-CONVERSATION 4

A: Is my hair dryer ready?
B: I'm afraid it isn't. We've been too busy. I'll try to have it ready for you tomorrow.

CONVERSATION PRACTICE

About the Conversation

1. What's wrong with the shower?   2. Why can't the guest take a hot bath?   3. Are there any towels?   4. Who is Charlie? What does he do at the hotel?   5. Why does the guest want to see the manager?   6. Where is the manager?   7. How many stars does the hotel have?   8. Why did the guest make a mistake?   9. Do you think he's going to stay there?

Situation 1

You are ready to leave your hotel and want to complain to the manager about the bill.

Ask to see the manager.
> The clerk says he / she is busy but will see you . . . (Say when.)

You are in a hurry because . . . (Say why.)
> The manager comes and asks what's the matter.

Tell him / her your bill is wrong.
> He / She asks to see it.

Tell him / her there has been a mistake and you have never . . .
> He / She apologizes and says there's another guest in the hotel who . . .

Situation 2

You are complaining to the hotel clerk about the service.

You have no pillow. Ask if he'll / she'll send one to you.
> He'll / she'll do it . . . (Say when.)

Also, it's cold and you only have one blanket.
> He / She can't give you another one because . . .

You'd like something hot to drink.
> Unfortunately he / she can't give you anything because . . .

Tell him / her what you think of the hotel and its service and what you intend to do about it.

SUMMARY OF NEW WORDS

VERBS: REGULAR

to apologize / apologized / apologized   to complain / complained / complained
to change / changed / changed

AUXILIARY VERB	PRONOUNS	ADJECTIVES					
will (won't)	none	broken	free	in a hurry	no	no good	ready

NOUNS					ADVERBS
blanket(s)	pillow(s)	receipt(s)	sheet(s)	towel(s)	in a minute
hair dryer(s)	pillowcase(s)	service	star(s)		right now

as soon as possible   not . . . at all   to do your best   to have something ready

EXERCISES

A. Ask and answer. Use Cue Book Chart 10. Start with *to put / this / 9 / on the bed / now.*

> STUDENT A: Will you put this blanket on the bed?
> STUDENT B: Yes, of course. I'll do it now.

1. to take / this / **10** / upstairs / now
2. to buy / a / **11** / this morning
3. to use / this / **12** / as soon as possible
4. to wash / this / **1** / after dinner
5. to clean / the / **2** / after lunch

6. to turn off / that / **3** / immediately
7. to lend me / your / **4** / right now
8. to complain about / this / **5** / in a minute
9. to wash / this / **6** / when I do the laundry
10. to put / the / **7** / in the closet / after I get up

B. Ask and answer. Use Cue Book Chart 6. Answer *ad lib.* Start with *Fernando / 4 / the yard.*

> STUDENT A: Will Fernando clean the yard?
> STUDENT B: (+) Yes, he will. He always does.
>   *or:* (−) No, he won't. He never does.

1. Maria / **5** / my pants
2. you *(sing.)* / **6** / my clothes
3. Mrs. Tanaka / **7** / her receipt
4. Mr. and Mrs. Ali / **8** / something nice
5. you *(pl.)* / **9** / the thief
6. Mrs. Davis / **10** / anything

7. the Tigers / **11** / the game
8. he / **12** / to give the baby his dinner
9. Mrs. Panos / **13** / the lamp
10. the children / **14** / the faucet
11. you *(pl.)* / **15** / suits
12. the cook / **1** / anything

Grammar Summary

1. Future Tense

AFFIRMATIVE (+)			NEGATIVE (−)		
I'll	*(I + will)*		I		
You'll	*(you + will)*		You		
He'll	*(he + will)*		He		
She'll	*(she + will)*	work.	She	**won't** *(will + not)*	work.
It'll	*(it + will)*		It		
We'll	*(we + will)*		We		
You'll	*(you + will)*		You		
They'll	*(they + will)*		They		

NOTE: *Will* + verb is the same as *going to* + verb.

QUESTION (?)		SHORT ANSWER (+)		SHORT ANSWER (−)	
Will	I you he she it we you they	work?	Yes,	I you he she it we you they	**will.**	No,	I you he she it we you they	**won't.**

NOTE: Tag questions are the same as in other tenses: *He'll* wash the dishes, **won't he?** / *I won't have to study,* **will I?**

2. *Adjectives:* No / Any *and Pronouns:* None / Any

There**'s no** hot water. = There **is none.** = There **isn't any** hot water. = There **isn't any.**
There **are no** towels. = There **are none.** = There **aren't any** towels. = There **aren't any.**

NOTE: We can't use *none* before a noun.

DEVELOPING YOUR SKILLS

A. Ask and answer. Use Cue Book Chart 7. Start with **9** / *after work.*

> STUDENT A: You won't forget to buy an umbrella, will you?
> STUDENT B: No, I won't. I'll do it after work.

1. **10** / downtown
2. **11** / this afternoon
3. **1** / before dinner
4. **2** / after lunch
5. **3** / immediately
6. **4** / this morning
7. **5** / those bills / today
8. **6** / tomorrow
9. **7** / when I get a haircut
10. **8** / in a minute
11. **9** / right now

B. Use *no, none,* or *any* in the following sentences.

1. There weren't ___ stars last night.
2. They don't give ___ receipts in that store.
3. There are ___ sheets on my bed!
4. I looked for some blankets in the closet, but there were ___.
5. Will you ask the manager if he has ___ clean towels?
6. There have been ___ accidents for a long time.
7. Who ate all the bread? There's ___ here.
8. Your neighbors can't lend you ___ money. They don't have ___.
9. There's ___ beer in the fridge. And ___ under the sink either. Do we have ___ wine?
10. Last year there were a few oranges on the trees, but this year there are ___.

Writing

Write a letter to Air Moronia to complain about their service. Example:

Air Moronia
P. O. Box 9346
Utopia,
MORONIA 812005

your address
date

Dear Sirs:

Tell why you are writing (to complain about . . .). Tell when you flew (give your flight number and the date). You were flying from . . . to . . . . The flight was late (say how late). When you boarded the plane there was somebody else in your seat. (Why was he / she there? What did you do?) Complain about the food, the flight attendants, etc. You wanted to sleep but you couldn't because . . . . You'll never fly Air Moronia again.

Yours truly,

your name

Talk About Yourself

1. Talk about the best / worst hotel you've ever stayed in.   2. Talk about the best / worst trip you've ever taken.   3. Have you ever complained about anything? What? Why? What happened after you complained?   4. What will you do after school today / tonight?   5. What will you do this weekend?   6. What will you do if it rains or snows tomorrow?

Test Yourself

Finish the sentences. Use the correct form *will* / *won't* + the right verb. (1 point each)

to apologize	to die	to get	to lie down	to wash
to complain	to fix	to get well	to taste	

1. If you don't like the service, I ___ to the manager immediately.
2. If you're really sorry, you ___ right now.
3. If the towels aren't clean enough, I ___ them for you.
4. If he doesn't breathe, he ___, ___ he?
5. If you don't take your medicine, you ___ quickly.
6. If you say the oranges are no good, I ___ them.
7. If they really want to rest, they ___ as soon as possible.
8. If your hair dryer is broken, my father ___ it when he comes home.
9. If you think she'll want to exchange it, we ___ a receipt.

Total Score_____

What to say . . .

LESSON 18

CONVERSATION

TOMMY: Look, Daddy! My ball has a hole in it.
              Could you fix it?

FATHER: Now don't cry! I'll fix it for you.

TOMMY: Will you?

5   FATHER: Yes, as soon as I've finished this.

TOMMY: Do you promise?

FATHER: I promise! Now I want you to go outside and
              ride your bike. OK?

TOMMY: But, Daddy, my bike's broken too!

10   LUCY: Daddy, Daddy! Peter wants me to go to the races
              with him. *(the telephone rings)* May I?

FATHER: Well , I . . . *(the phone rings again)* Will someone answer that phone? *(to Lucy)*
              Have you asked your mother?

LUCY: Yes. She just said, "Ask Daddy."

15   FATHER: Oh, all right. *(the doorbell rings)*

LUCY: I'll see who it is.

MOTHER: Darling, the Chens just called. They'd like us to have dinner with them Friday night.

FATHER: Friday night! But I have a . . . Danny! Will you turn down that music?

TOMMY: Daddy, you promised to fix my ball!

20   FATHER: I haven't forgotten, Tommy!

DANNY: Dad! I want you to listen to this new record. It's terrific!

MOTHER: Where are you going, darling?

FATHER: *(leaving the room)* To the North Pole!

TOMMY: Oh, boy! Can we go with you, Daddy?

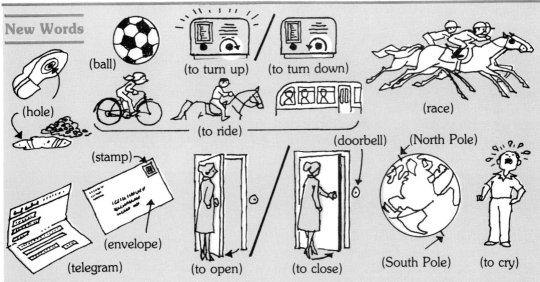

New Words

(ball) (hole) (to turn up) (to turn down) (to ride) (race) (stamp) (doorbell) (North Pole) (telegram) (envelope) (to open) (to close) (South Pole) (to cry)

DEFINITIONS

could: *can + would*; also past tense of *can: Could you fix this for me? I showed it to Mother, but she couldn't do it.*

filthy: very dirty.

fool: person who is not smart (not a nice word).

Let me / him / her / us / them: May I / he / she / we / they?

OK: all right.

to promise: to say that you certainly will or will not do something.

MINI-CONVERSATION 1

A: If you're going downtown, could you send this telegram for me?

B: Sure.

A: And I also need some stamps, if you don't mind.

B: Do you want me to buy anything else?

A: No, thanks. That's all.

MINI-CONVERSATION 2

A: Just look at my car! It's filthy.

B: Let me wash it for you, Dad.

A: Thanks.

• • •

B: Dad! I've finished. Come and have a look.

A: Oh, boy! Very nice.

B: Now can I borrow it?

MINI-CONVERSATION 3

A: What a beautiful song! Will you turn the radio up a little?

B: Of course.

A: Oh, it's just lovely.

B: Would you like me to buy the record?

A: Would you? I'd love to have it.

MINI-CONVERSATION 4

A: What do you want me to do, Boss?

B: I want you to pick up Buster and drive down to the old bridge.

A: What do you want us to do there, Boss?

B: What do you expect? I want you to kill him, you fool!

A: Oh. OK, Boss.

CONVERSATION PRACTICE

About the Conversation

1. What's wrong with Tommy's ball? 2. What does he want his father to do? 3. What does his father promise to do? 4. What does Tommy's father want him to do? 5. What does Peter want Lucy to do? 6. Do you think Lucy's mother wants her to go to the races? 7. What do the Chens want? 8. What does Danny's father want him to do? Why? 9. What does Danny want his father to do? 10. Where do you think the father is really going? Do you ever have the same kind of problem? What do you do?

Situation

Your boss wants you to do something for him / her.
    You ask what.
He / She tells you. Asks if you will do it.
    You say you will. Ask when / what time you have to do it.
He / She tells you and then tells you why he / she would like you to do it.
    You say OK.
He / She thanks you.

SUMMARY OF NEW WORDS

VERBS: REGULAR

to close / closed / closed   to promise / promised / promised
to cry / cried / cried   to turn up (down) / turned up (down) / turned up (down)

VERBS: IRREGULAR   **ADJECTIVES**

to ride / rode / ridden   filthy

NOUNS

ball(s)   envelope(s)   hole(s)   race(s)   stamp(s)
doorbell(s)   fool(s)   North / South Pole   song(s)   telegram(s)

PHRASES AND EXPRESSIONS

if you don't mind   Oh, boy!   OK   What (a) . . . !

EXERCISES

A. Ask and answer. Use Cue Book Chart 6. Start with *Mary / **2** / my stamps.*

    STUDENT A: What do you want Mary to do?
    STUDENT B: I want her to see my stamps.

1. Kiku / **3** / this hole
2. Mrs. Jones / **4** / my office
3. me / **5** / my shirt
4. the children / **6** / their hair
5. Abdul / **7** / I called him a fool

6. Maria / **8** / the songs for the show
7. us / **9** / the man who was complaining
8. my horse / **11** / the race
9. Bob / **12** / to send the telegram
10. Alexandra / **13** / the stereo

11. us / **14** / the radio
12. me / **15** / your sweater
13. Yoko and Pablo / **16** / their dinner while I'm riding my horse
14. Jane / **17** / her milk
15. me / **18** / to the market
16. them / **19** / the new song I wrote
17. your sister / **20** / the address on the envelope
18. us / **21** / with me to the North Pole
19. Danny / **22** / the ball to the baby
20. Tommy and Lucy / **23** / the doorbell

B. Say. Use Cue Book Chart 1. Start with *Mr. Moore / you / 2 / him.*

Mr. Moore would like you to dance with him.

1. Mr. Baker / me / **3** / my glass of wine
2. my father / us / **4** / his car
3. Mary and I / you / **5** / with us tonight
4. they / Mr. Bass / **6** / with them
5. Terry / me / **7** / his new record
6. Ann / her husband / **8** / a farm
7. our friends / us / **9** / cards
8. they / her / **10** / that popular new song
9. Mr. Wilson / you / **11** / next to him
10. Pete and Sue / me / **12** / at their house

C. Say. Use Cue Book Chart 8. Use *What a . . .* with count nouns and *What . . .* with plural and noncount nouns. Start with *1 / couch / chairs.*

What a comfortable couch! What comfortable chairs!

1. **2** / person / desserts
2. **3** / lemons / orange
3. **4** / language / homework
4. **5** / job / words
5. **6** / buildings / street
6. **7** / child / children
7. **8** / disease / holes
8. **9** / lamb / meal
9. **10** / woman / students
10. **11** / weather / day
11. **12** / prices / thermometer
12. **16** / bridge / gates
13. **17** / medicine / operation
14. **18** / morning / weather
15. **19** / bread / umbrella
16. **20** / models / cruise
17. **21** / patient / people

Grammar Summary

1. Polite Commands

If you want someone (not) to do something, but you don't know the person well, you ask:

Will / Would
Can / Could } **you (not) close** the door (please)?

If you know the person well, you can use *will / would* or *can / could* and you can also say:

I (don't) want you
I'd like you (not) } **to close** the door.

or: **(Don't) close** the door (please).

2. Volunteering

When you want to know if someone would like you to do something, but you don't know the person well, you ask:

Do you want me
Would you like me } **(not) to close** the door?

If you know the person well, you can also say:

I'll
Let me } **close** the door.

DEVELOPING YOUR SKILLS

1. Ask someone you know to answer the phone. 2. Tell your younger brother not to ride his bike so fast. 3. Ask your husband / wife to buy some bread. 4. Say you'll carry your friend's suitcase. 5. Ask your boss if he / she wants you not to leave early. 6. Tell your child to mail a package. 7. Say you'll lend someone you just met some change. 8. Ask your neighbor if he / she wants you to help him / her. 9. Ask someone you don't know to close the window.
10. Ask your teacher to have dinner with you. 11. Ask someone you just met if he / she would like you to do anything. 12. Say you'll find out the answer for someone you work with.
13. Ask someone you don't know to dial the phone for you. 14. Ask someone you've known all your life if he / she would like someone else to fix his / her jacket.

Talk About Yourself

1. What did your parents want you to be? 2. What didn't your parents use to like you to do? 3. Do you have children? Do they ask you to do things? What do you ask them to do? 4. What would you like your son / daughter to be?

Test Yourself

Complete the sentences with the following verbs. (1 point each)

to answer	to cry	to lie down	to ride	to turn up
to apologize	to examine	to promise	to taste	to win

1. Could you ___ the radio? I can't hear it.
2. I'd like you ___ not to leave the yard.
3. You're busy. Let me ___ the phone.
4. We really want you ___ the race.
5. Please don't ___ on top of the blanket.
6. The patient didn't want the nurse ___ him.

7. He wasn't nice to me at all and I want him ___.
8. Here's a handkerchief. I don't want you ___ anymore.
9. I hope there isn't too much salt in the soup. Would you ___ it for me?
10. I don't want you ___ your bike.

Total Score _____

What to say . . .

LESSON 19

CONVERSATION 1

ANTONIO: You've been to Utopia, haven't you?

SANDRA: Yes, I have. Richard and I were there on our honeymoon. Why do you ask?

ANTONIO: Well, I have to go there next month on business.

5 RICHARD: Just don't fly Air Moronia. They give you terrible service. You should go on Utopia Airlines. They're much better.

ANTONIO: I'll remember that. Is there anything else I should know?

10 SANDRA: Yes. You shouldn't keep any money in your pocket. Put it in your socks.

RICHARD: You really shouldn't carry any money at all. Use traveler's checks. They're much safer. You see, Utopia's a beautiful city, but it's full of thieves.

15 SANDRA: One other suggestion: Don't stay in a hotel downtown. It's much too dangerous at night.

RICHARD: Yes, you should try to get a room near the sea. It's a much nicer area and there are always police officers walking up and down on the beach.

20 SANDRA: What's the matter, Antonio? You look worried.

ANTONIO: I *am* worried! I'm not sure I should go there at all.

CONVERSATION 2

MARIA: The day after tomorrow is Alfred's birthday and I still don't have a present for him.

GLORIA: Why don't you get* him an electric razor?

MARIA: That's a good idea, but he already has one and I don't think he ever uses it.

5 GLORIA: How about some pajamas?

MARIA: The children gave him some on Father's Day and he hasn't worn them yet. . . . Maybe I'll buy him a tennis racket.

10 GLORIA: Does he play tennis?

MARIA: No, but he should. He's putting on too much weight.

GLORIA: Well, that will help him lose it.

---

*Here, *to get* = *to buy*.

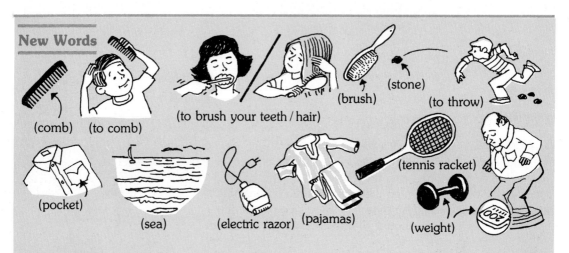

New Words

(comb)   (to comb)

(to brush your teeth / hair)

(brush)

(stone)

(to throw)

(pocket)

(sea)

(electric razor)

(pajamas)

(tennis racket)

(weight)

DEFINITIONS

Father's Day / Mother's Day: a special day when people give presents to their fathers / mothers.

full of: We use this expression to describe what something full has in it: *The bottle is full. It's full of water.*

to get: See Grammar Summary.

to keep: to put something somewhere and leave it there: *We keep our money in the bank.*

later: in the future; at a time after the time you're speaking about: *He brushed his teeth when he got up, but he combed his hair later.*

on business: for your business or your job: *I had to go to Spain on business.*

to put on / lose weight: to become fatter / thinner.

to shout: to call or to say something very loudly.

suggestion: idea for someone to do something.

up and down: to go to one place and then come back again; to do this many times. NOTE: **to jump up and down** = to jump in the air and come down again.

MINI-CONVERSATION 1

A: Why can't I go out?
B: Because you haven't done your homework.
A: I'll do it later.
B: No, you must do it now.

MINI-CONVERSATION 2

A: Tommy, what are you doing?
B: I'm smoking one of Daddy's cigarettes.
A: You shouldn't smoke. It isn't healthy.
B: Why can't I? You and Daddy do.

MINI-CONVERSATION 3

A: You look awful. What's wrong?
B: I have a terrible toothache.
A: Take one of your pain tablets.
B: I've already taken two, but it still hurts.
A: You should go to a dentist.
B: Yes, I think I will.

CONVERSATION PRACTICE

About Conversation 1

1. Why does Antonio want to know about Utopia?   2. How should Antonio go to Utopia?
Why?   3. What shouldn't he do with his money?   4. Should he carry bills and coins? Why?
What should he do instead?   5. Should he stay in a hotel downtown? Why not?   6. Where
should he stay? Why?   7. How does Antonio look? Why?   8. Do you think he'll go to Utopia?

About Conversation 2

1. What doesn't Maria have yet?   2. Should she give Alfred an electric razor? Why?
3. Should she get him some pajamas? Why?   4. What does she think she'll buy him?
5. Does Alfred play tennis?   6. Why should he play tennis?   7. Do you have Father's /
Mother's Day in your country? What do you usually do on that day?

Situation

You are telling a friend not to get married.

Your friend is in love. It was love at first sight.
  Ask about the boyfriend / girlfriend (what he's / she's like; how long they've known each
  other; how / when they met, etc.).
Your friend answers and tells you he / she doesn't have a job, etc.
  Ask where they are going to live and how they plan to live without any money.
Your friend tells you.
  Tell your friend why he / she shouldn't get married. He / She should . . .

SUMMARY OF NEW WORDS				
VERBS: REGULAR				
to brush / brushed / brushed		to comb / combed / combed		to shout / shouted / shouted
VERBS: IRREGULAR			**AUXILIARY VERBS**	**ADVERBS**
to keep / kept / kept	to throw / threw / thrown		should / shouldn't	later
NOUNS				
brush(es)	electric razor(s)	pocket(s)	stone(s)	tennis racket(s)
comb(s)	pajamas	sea(s)	suggestion(s)	weight(s)
Father's / Mother's Day				
PHRASES AND EXPRESSIONS				
full of on business	to look + *adj.*	to put on / to lose weight		up and down

EXERCISES

A. Use the right word or expression to finish the sentences.

1. When you go to bed you should wear *(pajamas / pockets)*.
2. After you wash your hair, don't forget *(to comb / to throw)* it.
3. Dad *(brushes his hair / shaves)* with an electric razor.
4. Those stones are terribly heavy. They're like *(seas / weights)*.
5. You should always *(keep / throw)* milk in the refrigerator.
6. Your jacket is filthy. It's full of dust. You should *(brush / comb)* it.
7. Don't talk so loudly. You don't need *(to cry / to shout)*.
8. A sea is *(bigger / smaller)* than a river.
9. Her father is awfully thin. He should *(put on / lose)* some weight.
10. You look tired. You *(should / shouldn't)* lie down later.
11. I have a *(comb / suggestion)*. Why don't you give Mom a hair dryer for Mother's Day?

B. Say. Use Cue Book Chart 5. Start with *Antonio / (−) to shave / his / 1.*

Antonio shouldn't shave his head.

1. you / (+) to comb / your / **2**
2. they / (+) to use / their / **3** *(pl.)*
3. the doctor / (+) to examine / your / **4**
4. the dentist / (+) to have a look at / her / **5**
5. you / (+) to brush / your / **6** *(pl.)* / after a meal
6. we / (−) to worry about / his / **7**
7. she / (+) to take off / her / **8** *(pl.)* / before she goes to bed
8. you / (+) to wash / your / **9**
9. you / (−) to complain about / your / **10**
10. they / (+) to examine / his / **11**
11. they / (+) to wash / their / **12** *(pl.)* / before they eat
12. he / (−) to use / that / **13**
13. she / (−) to wear / her / **14** *(pl.)*
14. I / (+) to keep / my / **15** / in my pocket
15. she / (+) to wash / those / **16** *(pl.)*
16. you / (−) to hit / your / **1**

C. Say. Use Cue Book Chart 10. Start with *I / to buy / her / 1.*

I'm going to buy her a saucepan.

1. we / to give / them / **2**
2. they / to lend / us / **3**
3. we / to get / her / **4**
4. she / to throw / me / **5**
5. I / to lend / him / **6**
6. Peter / to buy / me / **7**
7. Mrs. Jones / to get / them / **8**
8. the manager / to give / Mr. Van / **9**
9. Charlie / to bring / us / **10**
10. my wife / to buy / Bobby / **11**
11. Claude / to take / his boss / **12**
12. I / to get / my mother / **1**

Grammar Summary

1. *Auxiliary Verb:* Should / Shouldn't

Use *must / mustn't* to say what someone has to do:

You **mustn't** smoke. *(because you can't smoke here, because it will kill you, etc.)*
You **must** see your boss about that. *(because he's the only person who can help you, because if you don't you'll be in trouble, etc.)*

Use *should / shouldn't* to make suggestions:

You **shouldn't** smoke. *(because it's not healthy, you'll get sick, etc.)*
You **should** see your boss about that. *(because he'll help you, because he knows the answer, etc.)*

2. *Indirect Object Nouns and Pronouns*

The indirect object pronouns are the same as the direct object pronouns:

I → **me**
you → **you**
John / he → **him**
Mary / she → **her**
the thing / it → **it**

Mary and I / we → **us**
you → **you**
John and Mary / they → **them**

Note how we use them:

I want to buy a present **for Mary.**
I want to buy a present **for her.**   *or:*   I want to buy **Mary** a present.
I want to buy **her** a present.

In these sentences, *a present* is a direct object; *Mary* is an indirect object noun; *her* is an indirect object pronoun. When the indirect object noun or pronoun comes *before* the direct object, we don't use a preposition: I gave **the book to her.** → I gave **her the book.**

3. *The Verb* To Get

We use the verb *to get* in many ways:

to get =
- to look for and find: *I'm going to get a job.*
- to buy: *I got her this umbrella when I was in Utopia.*
- to have something that someone gave you or sent to you: *I got a post card from Alfred today.*

We also use *to get* in many expressions. Here are some you have learned:

to get on / off: to board / to leave: *He got on / off the bus at the corner.*
to get to: to arrive at: *We got to Athens at 10:00.*
to get married: to have a wedding: *We got married in a church.*
to get a haircut / shave: to go to a barber shop: *I need to get a haircut.*
to get sick / well: to become sick / well: *You certainly got well in a hurry.*
to get a disease: to have a disease: *I got the flu last week.*
to get up: not to lie down or sit anymore: *The children usually get up early.*

DEVELOPING YOUR SKILLS

Write the sentences using *should(n't)* and putting the indirect object first. Then say both sentences using indirect object pronouns. For example:

Don't give that electric razor to your boyfriend.
WRITE: *You shouldn't give your boyfriend that electric razor.*
SAY: *Don't give that electric razor to him.*
        You shouldn't give him that electric razor.

1. Don't buy those ugly pajamas for Dad.
2. Lend your comb to Mary.
3. Don't get that tennis racket for Alfred.
4. Don't give food to the animals.
5. Throw the ball to Fernando.
6. Don't sing any songs for Fred.
7. Get a ticket for Sally and me.
8. Don't give those brushes to the boys.
9. Take this envelope to Mr. Johnson.
10. Bring a chair for the president.

Reading

   Utopia, the capital of Moronia, is a very beautiful city, but unfortunately it has a lot of problems. The bus service is very bad—too many people and not enough buses. The subway is noisy and filthy and usually too full because so many people refuse to use the buses. The traffic[1] in the city is terrible. There are too many cars and the streets downtown are old and very
5 narrow. Because of this, people often get to work late.
   It is difficult to get a job in Utopia, and the cost of living is the highest in the country. The area near the sea still looks clean and pleasant, with two or three beautiful hotels and some very good restaurants. But the port is usually full of tourists, so the prices are high and most people who live in Utopia don't visit the area very often. It's just too expensive.
10   But robberies are the worst problem. Last year over 2,000 people were robbed. The authorities[2] are doing their best, and every day the newspapers and the TV and radio reporters have a new suggestion, but nothing helps and the problem is getting more and more serious.

About the Reading

1. Is Utopia an ugly city?   2. What's the bus service like? Why?   3. Why is the subway so full? What's it like?   4. Why do people often get to work late?   5. Is it easy to get a job in Utopia? 6. Is the cost of living low there?   7. Describe the area near the sea.   8. Why don't the Utopians visit the port very often?   9. What is getting more and more serious?   10. What are the authorities doing about it?   11. What do you think the authorities should do about the bus service? the subway? the traffic? jobs? the cost of living? robberies?

---

[1]Traffic = cars, buses, trucks, people, etc. going along a street or road.
[2]Authorities = people who work for a country, a city, etc. (the president, the prime minister, police officers, etc.).

Talk About Yourself

1. Does your town / country have problems like Utopia's? Talk about them.   2. What do you think is the worst problem in your town / country? What should the authorities do about it? Can they do anything?   3. What are the bus service, the subway, the traffic, jobs, the cost of living like in your town / country?

Test Yourself

First make a suggestion to these people. Then tell them what they have to do. (2 points each)

1.   2.   3.   4.   5.

What to say . . .

He should lose some weight.

People who live in glass houses shouldn't throw stones.

Song   DON'T

D
Don't send me presents on my wedding day
           G   D
Don't send me flowers when I die
                    Am
Don't write me letters when I go away
       G
Don't shout or cry
       D
5 Don't say good-by
G   A7 (2)
'Cause I'm leaving
D
You behind.

      D.   Am
Don't use your money on long distance calls
       G   D
Don't send unhappy telegrams
                    Am
10 Don't wait for me in summer, spring, or fall
       G
With empty arms.

                      D
Can't change my plans
       G   A7
It's too late now (2)
                D
To change my mind
       G   A7
'Cause I'm leaving (2)
D   Am
You behind.

           Am   D7
You must try to understand
       Bm   E7
You should find another man
       Am   D7   Am D7   G G7
There are many fish still swimming in the sea
                Am
Please forget me
           A7
Don't expect me
           D
'Cause I'm free.

15

20

Lesson 19   **one hundred thirty-five / 135**

LESSON 20

CONVERSATION

ELIZABETH: Hi, Margaret. How are things?

MARGARET: Terrific!

ELIZABETH: What's new?

MARGARET: I have a new boyfriend.

5 ELIZABETH: Really? So do I. I got tired of Wilbur. We never went out.

MARGARET: Neither did we. We just sat at home and watched TV.

ELIZABETH: So did Wilbur and I. And the few times we went out Wilbur used to talk about that dog of his all night.

10 Ugh! I hate dogs now!

MARGARET: Well, he wasn't as bad as Jeremy. Jeremy used to talk about his mother all the time. I don't even like mothers anymore!

ELIZABETH: But tell me about your new boyfriend.

15 MARGARET: Well, he loves to do things, so I rarely stay home.

ELIZABETH: I don't either. We've been everywhere together.

MARGARET: So have we—except on the weekend, of course. He goes home every weekend to see* his family. They live about 250 miles from here.

20 ELIZABETH: I never see my boyfriend during the week. He's too busy. He works all day and studies all night.

MARGARET: What does he look like?

ELIZABETH: Well, he's about six feet tall and very good-looking.

MARGARET: So is mine. He has blond hair and wears glasses.

25 I love men who wear glasses.

ELIZABETH: So do I. What does your boyfriend do?

MARGARET: He works with computers.

ELIZABETH: Oh, so does Roger!

MARGARET: Roger?

30 ELIZABETH: Yes, Roger Sly.

MARGARET: Ro- . . . ! But that's *my* boyfriend's name!

---

*Here, *to see* = *to visit*.

New Words

DEFINITIONS

blond: yellow. We usually use this word with hair.
during: from the time something starts to the time it finishes: *during the week, during the war*, etc.
except: but not: *I work every day except Sunday.*
foot: one meter = 3.28 feet.
to get + adj.: to become.
How are things?: How are you? How is everything?
like: We use this word to describe and compare: *It smells like fish. She ran the race like a champion.*
to look like: We use this expression to say maybe something will happen (*It looks like it's going to rain*) and to describe people and things (*She looks like an actress*).
mile: one kilometer = 0.62137 miles.
tired of: not liking something or someone anymore: *She got tired of her job / of working.*

MINI-CONVERSATION 1

A: I love music, but I just can't sing.
B: Neither can I.
A: Sometimes I sing in the shower, but my neighbors complain.
B: So did mine when I tried to learn to play the guitar. I used to play it when I was younger, but I was awful.
A: So was I. Now I just play my records and listen to the radio.
B: So do I.

MINI-CONVERSATION 2

A: Hi. How are things?
B: Fine. What's new with you?
A: Look at the pocket calculator my father just sent me. My dad's the greatest!
B: So's mine, except he can't give me presents like that. His salary isn't very good.
A: Neither is my dad's, but he still gives us expensive presents every week.
B: Really? What does your dad do?
A: Nothing lately. He's been in jail for the last few months.

CONVERSATION PRACTICE

About the Conversation

1. What's new with Margaret? 2. Why did Margaret get tired of Jeremy? 3. Why did Elizabeth get tired of Wilbur? 4. Does Margaret go out a lot now? When does she go out? 5. Does Elizabeth go out? When? 6. What does Elizabeth think her boyfriend is doing during the week? 7. What does Margaret think her boyfriend does on the weekend? 8. What does Margaret's boyfriend look like? What does he do? 9. What does Elizabeth's boyfriend look like? What does he do? 10. Who is Roger Sly? 11. What do you think is going to happen?

Situation

You are talking to someone about your vacation plans.

You've just bought a car and are going to drive to . . . *(Say where.)*
    He / She is too.
You were in . . . last year. *(Say where.)*
    He / She was too. He / She was there in . . . *(What month?)*
You were there in . . . *(What month?)* Describe the place, the weather, where you stayed, etc.
Say you met a lot of people. *(What were they like?)*
    He / She did too. He / She didn't buy many things because . . .
You didn't either, but this year you plan to buy a lot because . . .
    He / She does too.
You hope he / she has a good trip.

SUMMARY OF NEW WORDS

NOUNS		ADJECTIVES	PREPOSITIONS			CONJUNCTIONS
foot (feet)	mile(s)	blond	during	except	like	except

PHRASES AND EXPRESSIONS

to get + *adj.*	neither + *auxiliary verb* + *noun / pronoun*	tired of
How are things?	so + *auxiliary verb* + *noun / pronoun*	What's new?
to look like		

EXERCISES

Answer the questions.

1. Is a mile longer or shorter than a kilometer?   2. Is a foot longer or shorter than a meter?   3. Is your hair blond, brown, black, or gray?   4. What does your teacher look like? Describe him / her.   5. What would you like to do when you get old?   6. What have you learned during the year in your English class? Have you enjoyed it? Why?   7. Are you tired of going to school? Is the work easy enough or is it too hard?   8. What days do you work? (Use *except* in your answer.)   9. What's new with you? How are things?

Grammar Summary

1. *Prepositions:* For / During

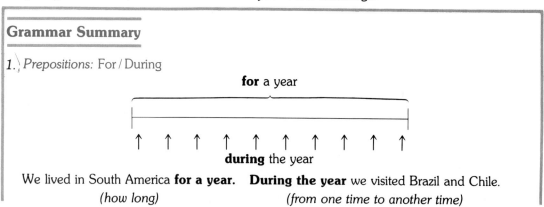

We lived in South America **for a year.**   **During the year** we visited Brazil and Chile.
    (how long)   *(from one time to another time)*

NOTE: The preposition *for* often has a number after it: *I've worked here for three years.*

2. *Conjunctions:* So / Too / Neither / Not . . . Either

AFFIRMATIVE (+)

A: I'm glad. / I'm walking. / I'm going to work.
B: So am I. / I am too.

A: I was happy. / I was eating.
B: So was I. / I was too.

A: I like to eat.
B: So do I. / I do too.

A: My sister planned to study.
B: So did mine. / Mine did too.

A: I used to read a lot.
B: So did I. / I did too.

A: I've been to England.
B: So have I. / I have too.

A: I can speak English.
B: So can I. / I can too.

A: I could read when I was five.
B: So could I. / I could too.

A: I'll leave now.
B: So will I. / I will too.

A: His family would like to travel.
B: So would mine. / Mine would too.

A: I should go to bed.
B: So should I. / I should too.

A: I must get a job soon.
B: So must I. / I must too.

NEGATIVE (−)

A: I'm not cold / walking / going to work.
B: Neither am I. / I'm not either.

A: I wasn't hungry / eating.
B: Neither was I. / I wasn't either.

A: I don't intend to work.
B: Neither do I. / I don't either.

A: My sister didn't do her homework.
B: Neither did mine. / Mine didn't either.

A: I didn't use to read very much.
B: Neither did I. / I didn't either.

A: I've never been to France.
B: Neither have I. / I haven't either.

A: I can't speak French.
B: Neither can I. / I can't either.

A: I couldn't read when I was four.
B: Neither could I. / I couldn't either.

A: I won't leave now.
B: Neither will I. / I won't either.

A: I wouldn't like to do that.
B: Neither would I. / I wouldn't either.

A: I shouldn't eat so much.
B: Neither should I. / I shouldn't either.

A: I mustn't forget to get up early.
B: Neither must I. / I mustn't either.

NOTE: We can use any noun or any subject pronoun *(I, you, he, she,* etc.) or possessive pronoun *(mine, yours, his, hers,* etc.) in these statements.

DEVELOPING YOUR SKILLS

A. Use *for* or *during* in the following sentences.

1. We had to drive 500 miles. I got terribly tired ____ the trip.
2. Jeremy brushes his teeth ____ ten minutes every day.
3. My aunt lived in France ____ the war.
4. I've played the guitar ____ more than twenty years.
5. I've learned a lot ____ this year.
6. The children shouted ____ the game.
7. Uncle George kept that letter ____ thirty years.
8. The students couldn't talk ____ the test.

9. Our boss was in bed with the flu ____ ten days.
10. We were only there ____ a few minutes.

B. Answer. Use Cue Book Chart 1. Start with *I love to / 1 / with people / he.*

STUDENT A: I love to argue with people.
STUDENT B: So does he.

1. they liked to / **2** / with him / she
2. I'll / **3** / some / I
3. she can / **4** / a bus / they
4. I'm / **5** / an awfully big breakfast / they
5. I usually / **6** / on vacation / we
6. I should / **7** / to the professor / everyone else
7. you must / **8** / her a present / her parents
8. I could / **9** / tennis when I was younger / I
9. he can / **10** / well / you
10. I want to / **11** / in that corner / they
11. my brother used to / **12** / a lot / mine
12. I've / **13** / too many cigarettes / we
13. I'd like to / **14** / to the prime minister / his wife
14. they're / **15** / at the bus stop / Alexandra
15. you should / **16** / to your boss / she
16. I'm / **17** / for the others / I
17. I've / **18** / a mile already / he
18. I should / **19** / harder / we
19. we must / **20** / to our friends soon / they

C. Use Cue Book Chart 2. Start with *I didn't have any / 6 / with my meat / I.*

STUDENT A: I didn't have any tomatoes with my meat.
STUDENT B: Neither did I.

1. we aren't going to have any / **7** / for dessert / we
2. Mrs. Tanaka didn't find any / **8** / at the market / my mother
3. Mr. Panos doesn't like / **9** / in his salad / Mr. Chen
4. we haven't had / **10** / for a long time / we
5. my mother isn't cooking / **11** / tonight / mine
6. I never eat / **12** / I
7. we can't get / **13** / anymore / we
8. my sister won't eat / **14** / I
9. we couldn't eat all our / **15** / the others
10. they wouldn't like / **16** / we
11. our children didn't use to like / **17** / ours
12. I shouldn't eat / **18** / I
13. we haven't bought any / **1** / Dad
14. we won't complain about the / **2** / she
15. I can't taste the / **3** / I

Reading

ELIZABETH *(angry):*

The next time I see Roger I'm going to break his neck. Who does he think he is? He was actually going out with my best friend and me at the same time! He used to tell me he loved me so much. And he was always so busy during the week. He said he was trying to make a lot of money for our future. And then he had to study every night. Oh! What a fool I was! I worried about him because he was

MARGARET *(sad):*

Oh, well, I guess there's nothing I can do. It's a shame because I really liked him. But still, it's better to find out now than later. I just can't understand why he did it. What's wrong with somebody like that? He really must have serious problems. The next time I see him I'm going to tell him he shouldn't do this to people. I certainly learned something; so will he, I hope. Well, there are a lot of fish in the

10   working so hard. I even apologized when I thought I was seeing him too often. I'll kill him! He'll never do this again to anybody else!

sea. I'm sure I'll find someone much better than he was . . . . Well, that's life, I guess. But it sure was nice while it lasted.   10

About the Reading

Which woman do you think is right? Why? What do you think will really happen?

Writing

Use the Reading to write the conversations between Elizabeth and Roger and Margaret and Roger *or* write the letters they will send him *or* write one conversation and one letter.

Talk About Yourself

1. What does your father / mother / brother / sister look like?   2. Have you ever had a boyfriend / girlfriend like Roger Sly? Do you know anyone who has? Talk about it.   3. Do you know anyone like Wilbur or Jeremy (see the Conversation, page 136, lines 5–13)? Talk about them.

Test Yourself

What do you say in these situations? (1 point each)

1. Someone says: "How are things?" *(Just fine. / What's new?)*
2. Someone says: "Do you mind if I smoke?" *(Bless you. / Not at all.)*
3. Someone says: "I think he's wrong." *(Neither do I. / So do I.)*
4. Somebody makes a mistake. *(Congratulations. / That's all right.)*
5. A friend of yours has had an accident. *(Oh, I'm so sorry. / Too bad.)*
6. Somebody wants to speak to your mother on the phone. *(Hold the line, please. / Forget it!)*
7. A neighbor can't find her little girl. *(Let's go for a walk. / Don't worry.)*
8. You arrive home at night and you find the door open. *(Really? / That's strange.)*
9. A friend is arriving after a long trip. *(It was love at first sight. / I've missed you.)*
10. The service was very bad and you left. *(I got tired of waiting. / I couldn't turn right.)*

Total Score _____

What to say . . . .

She sings like a bird.

He swims like a fish.

I ate like a horse.

I felt like a fool.

Test Yourself: Answers

LESSON 1, PAGE 5

1. *A:* Would you like *B:* I'd like   2. alone
3. phone number   4. welcome   5. *A:* How are
you? *B:* How are   6. Anything   7. *A:* This is
B: Nice (*or:* Pleased) to meet you.   8. *A:* aren't I
B: Why *A:* Because   9. How do you do?
10. What time is it?

LESSON 2, PAGE 11

1. Normally we get up early (*or:* late) but yesterday
we got up late (*or:* early).   2. When did you last
read a good book?   3. Peggy's parents rarely called
her because they didn't have a phone.   4. I'm
afraid I forgot to buy some potatoes.   5. Kiku sold
a very interesting story to the newspapers.

LESSON 3, PAGE 18

1. them   2. us   3. me   4. it   5. him   6. excited
7. fat   8. fresh   9. thirsty   10. strong

LESSON 4, PAGE 28

Write the sentences, then talk to your teacher.

LESSON 5, PAGE 35

1. where the barber shop is   2. wrong   3. Not at
all.   4. over   5. across   6. where the supermarket
is   7. May I ask   8. floor / opposite   9. parking lot

LESSON 6, PAGE 42

1. band   2. yet / Maybe   3. high   4. lucky   5. so
6. on top of   7. area   8. old-fashioned / boring

LESSON 7, PAGE 51

1. well   2. softly   3. slowly   4. soft (*or:* nice, good,
etc.) / delicious (*or:* good, inexpensive, etc.)   5. terribly (*or:* very badly, etc.)   6. hard   7. quietly
8. careful   9. immediately (*or:* now, today, etc.)

LESSON 8, PAGE 58

1. He didn't earn very much so he left his job.
2. Her long stories really bore me.   3. Your uncle
became the personnel manager, didn't he?   4. Her
father used to hit them, didn't he?   5. Mrs. Drake is
a very nice person, isn't she?

LESSON 9, PAGE 66

1. Nothing   2. anyone   3. everybody   4. something   5. somewhere   6. Somebody   7. anywhere   8. everywhere   9. anything   10. Nowhere

LESSON 10, PAGE 74

was walking / saw / was lying / tried / was choosing /
woke up / left / wrote / thanked / didn't sign

LESSON 11, PAGE 81

1. c   2. d   3. h   4. f   5. i   6. a   7. b   8. e   9. j
10. g

LESSON 12, PAGE 88

1. e   2. i   3. h   4. j   5. b   6. d   7. c   8. g   9. a
10. f

LESSON 13, PAGE 95

Write the sentences, then talk to your teacher.

LESSON 14, PAGE 102

Write the sentences, then talk to your teacher.

LESSON 15, PAGE 111

1. When did Buster become a robber?   2. How
long has he been a robber?   3. Has he ever been
in jail?   4. When did he get married to Flo?
5. How long have they been married?

LESSON 16, PAGE 116

1. quickly / more quickly   2. uncomfortable / the
most uncomfortable   3. more famous / the most
famous   4. harder / the hardest   5. ugly / the ugliest
6. bad / worse   7. better / the best   8. fast / the
fastest   9. worse / the worst   10. beautiful / less
beautiful

LESSON 17, PAGE 123

1. I'll complain   2. you'll apologize   3. I'll wash
4. he'll die / won't   5. won't get well   6. won't taste
7. they'll lie down   8. will fix   9. we'll get

LESSON 18, PAGE 128

1. turn up   2. to promise   3. answer   4. to win
5. lie down   6. to examine   7. to apologize   8. to
cry   9. taste   10. to ride

LESSON 19, PAGE 135

Write the sentences, then talk to your teacher.

LESSON 20, PAGE 141

1. Just fine.   2. Not at all.   3. So do I.   4. That's
all right.   5. Oh, I'm so sorry.   6. Hold the line,
please.   7. Don't worry.   8. That's strange.
9. I've missed you.   10. I got tired of waiting.

Vocabulary

The following vocabulary includes all words taught in Book II, plus all verbs and subject pronouns taught in Book I. The number following each entry refers to the lesson in which that word was presented. A Roman numeral (I) following an entry means that the word was presented in Book I.

accident(s) (10)
ache(s) (15)
across (5)
actually (13)
address(es) (1)
after *prep.* (I); *conj.* (15)
   to look — (2)
again (11)
age(s) (11)
agency *see* real estate
   agency, travel
   agency
agent *see* travel agent
ago (2)
air (16)
all (4)
   — of (4)
   — the time (3)
   not at — (17)
   that's (quite) — right
     (13)
along (5)
already (12)
also (4)
announcer(s) (3)
another *pron. & adj.*
   (11)
to answer / —ed / —ed
   (7;12)
   to — the phone (11)
answer(s) (7)
anybody (9)
anymore (7)
anyone (9)
anywhere (4)
to apologize / —d / —d
   (17)
application(s) (7)
to apply / —ied / —ied
   (for) (7;12)
appointment(s) (7)
area(s) (6)
to argue / —d / —d (I;12)
arm(s) (10)
to arrive / —d / —d (I;12)
as + *adj.* / *adv.* + as
   (14)

— soon — possible
   (17)
ashtray(s) (12)
to ask / —ed / —ed (7;12)
   May I / we — (3;5)
asleep (10)
atchoo! (16)
ate *see* to eat
aunt(s) (8)
awful (9)
awfully (13)

baby (babies) (12)
back: to come — (12)
back(s) (15)
backache(s) (15)
badly (7)
the Bahamas (3)
ball(s) (18)
band(s) (6)
barber shop(s) (5)
to be / was (were) / been
   (I;12)
became *see* to become
because (I)
   — of (15)
to become / became / be-
   come (8;12)
bee(s) (14)
been *see* to be
before *prep.* (I); *conj.*
   (15)
(the) day — yester-
   day (2)
to begin / began / begun
   (11;12)
besides (11)
best (16)
   — man (6)
   to do your — (17)
better (14)
bill(s) (4); *money* (11)
birthday(s) (4)
   Happy B— (4)
blanket(s) (17)
Bless you! (16)

blond (20)
to board / —ed / —ed
   (I;3;12)
body (bodies) (15)
boiled (4)
to bore / —d / —d (8;12)
boring (6)
born: to be — (8)
to borrow / —ed / —ed
   (something from
   someone) (11;
   12)
boss(es) (12)
both *pron.* (12)
bought *see* to buy
boxing (9)
boy: Oh, —! (18)
brand(s) (16)
bread (4)
to break / broke / broken
   (10;12)
breath(s) (16)
to breathe / —d / —d (15)
bride(s) (6)
bridesmaid(s) (6)
bridge(s) (5)
to bring / brought / brought
   (4;12)
broiled (4)
broke *see* to break
broken *adj.* (17); *see*
   also to break
brought *see* to bring
to brush / —ed / —ed (19)
brush(es) (19)
   tooth—(es) (16)
bus stop(s) (5)
business(es) (7)
   on — (19)
to buy / bought / bought
   (I;12)

to call / —ed / —ed (2;12)
call(s) (11)
calling: Thanks for —
   (13)

came *see* to come
can('t) / could(n't) *aux.*
   verb (7)
   — I take your order?
     (4)
   What — I / we do for
     you? (7)
careful (7)
   —ly (7)
careless (7)
   —ly (7)
carrot(s) (4)
to carry / —ied / —ied
   (11;12)
to cash / —ed / —ed (I;2;
   12)
to catch / caught / caught
   (10;12)
century (centuries) (4)
certainly (4)
champion(s) (9)
to change / —d / —d (17)
change *money* (11)
changeable (14)
channel(s) (3)
cheap (14)
check: traveler's —(s)
   (11)
to check in / —ed / —ed
   (I;3;12)
Cheers! (1)
cheesecake (4)
chemistry (5)
chest(s) (15)
to choose / chose / chosen
   (10;12)
chopstick(s) (4)
chose(n) *see* to choose
church(es) (5)
class(es) (5)
to clean / —ed / —ed (12)
cleaner(s): vacuum —
   (16)
to close / —d / —d (18)
closed *adj.* (6)
cloth(s) (11)
cloudy (14)

cocktail(s): shrimp —
(4)
coin(s) (11)
cold(s) (15)
collect adj. (11)
to comb / —ed / —ed (19)
comb(s) (19)
to come / came / come
(I;12)
to — back (12)
to — from (I)
comfortable (14)
company (companies)
(7)
to compare / —d / —d
(14)
to complain / —ed / —ed
(17)
congratulations! (3)
control: passport — (3)
to cook / —ed / —ed
(I;2;12)
corner(s) (5)
corridor(s) (5)
to cost / cost / cost (14)
the cost of living (14)
cough(s) (15)
could(n't) aux. verb (7)
— you . . . ? (4)
— you tell me / us
(5)
the country (14)
course(s) at meals (4)
cow(s) (11)
crazy (9)
cried see to cry
cruise(s) (3)
to cry / —ied / —ied (18)

to dance / —d / —d (I;2;
12)
dancing: to go — (2)
dangerous (14)
darling n. (2)
date(s) (13)
day:
Father's (Mother's)
Day (19)
(the) — before yes-
terday (2)
dear: oh, —! (12)
to declare / —d / —d (I;
12)
department(s) (11)

to describe / —d / —d (12)
to dial / —ed / —ed (11;
12)
diamond(s) (10)
did(n't) see to do
to die / —d / —d (8;12)
different (4)
— from (15)
difficult (14)
disease(s) (15)
to get a — (15)
dish(es) (12)
to do (the) —es (13)
to do / did / done (I;12);
aux. verb (I)
How — you —? (1)
to — (the) dishes
(13)
to — homework (13)
to — (the) house-
work (13)
to — (the) laundry
(13)
to — your best (17)
What can I / we —
for you? (7)
does(n't) see to do
done see to do
don't see to do
doorbell(s) (18)
down (5)
to lie — (15)
to sit — (7)
to turn — (18)
up and — (19)
drank see to drink
to drink / drank / drunk
(I;12)
drink(s) (3)
to drive / drove / driven
(I;12)
drive(s) (13)
to go for a — (13)
driven see to drive
driver(s) (5)
—'s license(s) (11)
drove see to drive
drunk see to drink
dry (14)
dryer(s): hair — (17)
duck (4)
during (20)
dust (16)
duty-free (3)

each other pron. (11)
ear(s) (10)
earache(s) (15)
to earn / —ed / —ed (7;
12)
earring(s) (10)
easy (14)
to eat / ate / eaten (I;12)
to — out (4)
economical (16)
electric (13)
— razor(s) (19)
to enjoy / —ed / —ed
(3;12)
enormous (6)
enough (4)
envelope(s) (18)
estate see real estate
even adv. (9)
ever (10)
every + time (15)
everybody (6)
everyone (9)
everywhere (9)
to examine / —d / —d
(15)
except (20)
to exchange / —d / —d
(11;12)
excited (3)
exciting (9)
to expect / —ed / —ed
(7;12)

failure(s) (12)
famous (8)
fantastic (6)
fast adj. & adv. (7)
Father's Day (19)
faucet(s) (12)
to feel / felt / felt (13)
feet see foot
felt see to feel
fever (15)
few: a — pron. & adj.
(9)
fight(s) (14)
to fill out / —ed / —ed
(7;12)
filthy (18)
to find / found / found
(6;12)

to — out (14)
finger(s) (10)
to finish / —ed / —ed
(I;12)
first: love at — sight
(16)
to fish / —ed / —ed (I;2;
12)
to fix / —ed / —ed (12)
flew see to fly
floor(s) (5)
flower(s) (13)
flown see to fly
the flu (15)
to fly / flew / flown (I;3;
12)
following (8)
fool(s) (18)
foot (feet) (9); meas-
ure (20)
foreigner(s) (11)
to forget / forgot / forgotten (2;12)
— it! (11)
fork(s) (4)
form(s) (7)
fortunately (13)
found see to find
free (17)
French fries (4)
fried (4)
friend: a — of (mine,
etc.) (1)
friendly (14)
fries: French — (4)
frying pan(s) (16)
full (I)
— of (19)
to have your hands
— (4)
funny (9)
future (6)

game(s) (15)
gave see to give
German n. & adj. (7)
Germany (7)
to get / got / gotten (2;12)
to — + adj. (20)
to — a disease (15)
to — a haircut /
shave (13)
to — a job (8)
to — married (6)

ready (17)
  to have something
    — (17)
real estate agency
  (agencies) (5)
really (2)
receipt(s) (17)
receiver(s) (11)
reception(s) (6)
receptionist(s) (5)
to refuse / —d / —d (13)
regards (2)
  to send my (your,
    etc.) — (2)
relaxed (14)
to remember / —ed /
    —ed (9;12)
to rent / —ed / —ed (I;3;
    12)
to report / —ed / —ed
    (I;2;12)
to rest / —ed / —ed (I;3;
    12)
ridden see to ride
to ride / rode / ridden (18)
right n., adj. & adv. (5)
  — now (17)
  to come / go — in
    (7)
to ring / rang / rung (11;
    12)
ring(s) (10)
road(s) (5)
roast(ed) (4)
to rob / —bed / —bed
    (10;12)
robbed: to be — (10)
robber(s) (10)
robbery (robberies)
    (10)
rode see to ride
to run / ran / run (I;3;12)
rung see to ring

sadly (7)
safe (14)
said see to say
saké (12)
salary (salaries) (7)
sales (11)
salt (11)
same (2)
sang see to sing
sat see to sit

sauce(s) (4)
saucepan(s) (16)
saw see to see
to say / said / said (8;12)
school(s) (I)
  high —(s) (8)
  primary —(s) (8)
sea(s) (19)
to see / saw / seen (I;12)
  Good to — you (7)
seen see to see
to sell / sold / sold (I;2;12)
to send / sent / sent (2;12)
  to — my (your, etc.)
    regards (2)
serious (13)
service (17)
to shave / —d / —d (13)
shave(s) (13)
  to get a — (13)
she (I)
  —'d (1)
  —'ll (17)
  —'s (I)
sheep (sheep) (11)
sheet(s) (17)
shop(s): barber — (5)
shorthand (7)
  to take — (7)
should(n't) aux. verb
    (19)
shoulder(s) (15)
to shout / —ed / —ed (19)
to show / —ed / shown
    (I;12)
show(s) (3)
shown see to show
shrimp (4)
  — cocktail(s) (4)
sick: to get — (15)
sight: love at first —
    (16)
to sign / —ed / —ed (10;
    12)
since conj. & prep. (15)
to sing / sang / sung (I;12)
to sit / sat / sat (I;12)
  to — down (7)
to sleep / slept / slept (I;
    12)
slept see to sleep
slow (7)
  —ly (7)
smart (14)
to smell / —ed / —ed (16)

smell(s) (16)
to smoke / —d / —d (I;2;
    12)
snail(s) (4)
snake(s) (4)
to sneeze / —d / —d (16)
to snow / —ed / —ed (I;
    12)
so adv. of degree (7);
    conj. (8)
  I don't think — (6)
  I guess / hope — (6)
  — + aux. verb +
    noun / pron.
    (20)
soap (3)
soft (7)
  —ly (7)
sold see to sell
somebody (9)
someday (9)
someone (7)
somewhere (4)
song(s) (18)
soon (13)
  as — as possible
    (17)
.sour (14)
South Pole (18)
to speak (to) / spoke /
    spoken (I;12)
special (4)
spoon(s) (4)
square (6)
stamp(s) (18)
to stand / stood / stood (I;
    12)
star(s) (17)
  movie —(s) (9)
to start / —ed / —ed (I;2;
    12)
to stay / —ed / —ed (I;12)
steak(s) (4)
to steal / stole / stolen
    (10;12)
stole(n) see to steal
stomach(s) (15)
stomachache(s) (15)
stone(s) (19)
stood see to stand
stop(s): bus — (5)
strange (14)
studio(s) (6)
to study / —ied / —ied
    (I;12)

subway(s) (5)
success(es) (12)
suddenly (10)
suggestion(s) (19)
sun (3)
sung see to sing
supermarket(s) (5)
sure interj. (5); adj. (6)
surprise(s) (6)
swam see to swim
sweet (14)
to swim / swam / swum
    (I;3;12)
swim(s) (13)
  to go for a — (13)
swimming pool(s) (3)
swum see to swim

tablet(s) (15)
to take / took / taken (I;
    12)
  Can I — your order?
    (4)
  to -- a bath / show-
    er (I)
  to — a / the train
    (bus, etc.) (5)
  to — a vacation (6)
  to — off planes (3);
    clothes (15)
  to — photographs (I)
  to — shorthand (7)
  to — someone's
    temperature (15)
to talk / —ed / —ed (I;2;
    12)
to taste / —d / —d (16)
taste (16)
tasty (14)
teeth see tooth
telegram(s) (18)
to tell / told / told (5;12)
  Could you — me /
    us (5)
temperature(s) (15)
  to take someone's —
    (15)
tennis racket(s) (19)
tequila (12)
terribly (7); adv. of
    degree (8)
than: more / less +
    adj. / adv. + —
    (14)

to thank / —ed / —ed
(10;12)
thanks for calling (13)
that *pron. & adj.* (I);
relative pron. (9)
them (3)
thermometer(s) (15)
they (I)
—'d (1)
—'ll (17)
—'re (I)
things: How are —?
(20)
to think / thought / thought
(I;12)
I (don't) — so (6)
to — of (I)
thought *see* to think
threw *see* to throw
through (3)
to throw / threw / thrown
(19)
time: all the — (3)
tired of (20)
told *see* to tell
tomato(es) (4)
took *see* to take
tooth (teeth) (10)
toothache(s) (15)
toothbrush(es) (16)
toothpaste (16)
top: on — (of) (6)
total *adj.* (6)
tourist(s) (8)
towel(s) (17)
traffic light(s) (5)
to travel / —ed / —ed
(I;12)
travel agency (agen-
cies) (3)
travel agent(s) (3)
traveler's check(s) (11)
treatment(s) (15)
tried *see* to try

truck(s) (6)
to try / tried / tried (10;12)
to turn / —ed / —ed (5)
to — on / off (12)
to — up / down (18)
to type / —d / —d (7;12)

umbrella(s) (13)
uncle(s) (8)
uncomfortable (15)
to understand / under-
stood / under-
stood (7;12)
to — why (14)
unfortunately (13)
university (universities)
(5)
up (5)
to get — (I)
to hang — (11)
to pick — (2)
to turn — (18)
to wake — (10)
us (3)
to use / —d / —d (3;12)
— to + *verb* (7)
usher(s) (6)

vacation(s): to take (a)
— (6)
vacuum cleaner(s) (16)
veal (4)
to visit / —ed / —ed (14)

to wait (for) / —ed / —ed
(I;12)
to wake up / woke up /
waked up (10;
12)
to walk / —ed / —ed (I;
12)

walk(s) (13)
to go for a — (13)
wallet(s) (10)
to want / —ed / —ed
(I;2;12)
was / were *see* to be
to wash / —ed / —ed (12)
washing machine(s)
(13)
to watch / —ed / —ed
(I;12)
water (12)
we (I)
—'d (1)
—'ll (17)
—'re (I)
to wear / wore / worn (I;
3;12)
wedding(s) (6)
to weigh / —ed / —ed
(9;12)
weight(s) (19)
to lose / put on —
(19)
well *interj.* (I); *adj.* (2);
adv. (7)
to be — (2)
to get — (15)
well-done (4)
went *see* to go
were *see* to be
wet (14)
what . . . ! / what
a . . . ! (18)
I('m) / You('re), etc.
—!? (2)
while (10)
whiskey (15)
who? (I); *relative pron.*
(9)
whole (16)
wide (14)
will / won't (17)
to win / won / won (9;12)

with: What's wrong —?
(15)
without (9)
woke up *see* to wake
up
won *see* to win
won't *see* will
word(s) (7)
wore *see* to wear
to work / —ed / —ed
(I;2;12)
worker(s) (7)
worn *see* to wear
to worry / —ied / —ied
(12)
worse (14)
worst (16)
would(n't) (1;4)
to write / wrote / written
(I;12)
writer(s) (8)
written *see* to write
wrong *adj. & adv.* (5)
What's — (with)?
(15)
wrote *see* to write

yesterday: (the) day
before — (2)
yet (6)
you *subject pron.* (I);
sing. obj. pron.
(2); *pl. obj.
pron.* (3)
Bless — (16)
See — (I)
thank — (I)
—'d (1)
—'ll (17)
—'re (I)

Index

Numbers refer to lessons, not pages.